GIFTS *for* YOUR SOUL

Also by Sheila Walsh

Honestly

GIFTS *for*
YOUR SOUL

a book of daily devotions

SHEILA WALSH

ZondervanPublishingHouse
Grand Rapids, Michigan

A Division of HarperCollins*Publishers*

Gifts for Your Soul
Copyright © 1997 by Sheila Walsh

Requests for information should be addressed to:

⚏ ZondervanPublishingHouse
Grand Rapids, Michigan 49530

Library of Congress Cataloging-in-Publication Data

Walsh, Sheila, 1956–.
    Gifts for your soul : a book of daily devotions / Sheila Walsh.
       p.   cm.
    ISBN: 0-310-20975-7 (hardcover)
    1. Meditations 2. Devotional calendars. 3. Christian life. 4. Spiritual life—
Christianity. 5. Walsh, Sheila, 1956–   . I. Title.
BV48432.2.M495 1997
242'—dc21   97-9222
                                        CIP

This edition printed on acid-free paper and meets the American National
Standards Institute Z39.48 standard.

Published in association with the literary agency of Wolgemuth & Hyatt, Inc.,
8012 Brooks Chapel Road, #243, Brentwood, Tennessee 37027.

Interior design by Sue Vandenberg-Koppenol

Printed in the United States of America

---

97 98 99 00 01 02 03 04 /❖ DH/ 10 9 8 7 6 5 4 3

*This book is dedicated with all my love
to my husband, Barry, and my son, Christian—
True Gifts to my Soul.*

CONTENTS

ACKNOWLEDGMENTS

I would like to express my deepest gratitude to Ann Spangler, Evelyn Bence, and Mary McNeil for their enormous contribution in editing this book. I love to write, but my thoughts would be much more clumsy and cluttered without these gifted women.

INTRODUCTION

I hear a muffled voice at times,
*   it's carried on the wind.*
I turn toward the melody.
*   I know this ancient hymn,*
the song is so familiar,
*   its words like liquid gold.*
I start to sing
*   the anthem of the soul.*

I sensed I had been whistling a tune for some time. I didn't always remember the whole melody, but I found the theme haunting, and I was drawn back to it again and again. It was something that stirred deep inside me, and when I was with some of my closest friends the melody was stronger than ever. Then one day I opened a parcel and began to read the book it contained: *The Jesus I Never Knew* by Philip Yancey. I intended to read for only a while. I had errands to run and mail to post, but I read on and on. Yancey put words to the melody that had been stirring in my soul for so long. I cried as I read. I think I cried from pure relief. It was wonderful to hear the ache from my own heart poured so eloquently onto paper by a fellow traveler. The questions Yancey raised are the questions I am asking: What is the purpose of my life? How can I sing that purposeful song to a world that seems to hate the tune? How can I know God? How do I lay aside my twentieth-century glasses and be in relationship with the true Christ? Why is it so hard to remain at peace?

Why do I feel torn in two—between a song that is eternal and one that is so earthbound and transitory?

I write this book, not because I have great answers but because I have a great hunger to know God, to learn how to love, to care for the part of my life that is eternal. I have spent so many years working on the external surface of my life that my inner life is weed-choked and overgrown.

I feel as if I am starting to sing this song at midnight; it is like a dark night with few stars to light the path. Occasionally the moon peeps out from behind a cloud and a ribbon of gold illumines the next few steps, but most of the journey is shadowy and I have to step carefully and slowly.

The new anthem of my soul is drawing me to the greatest adventure offered to a man or woman: to discover who we are in Christ, where are we going, and how to walk with each other. As a child, I was told that who I am in the dark with God is who I really am. My question was, "But who is going to see *that?*"

It has taken me a long time to understand that I was asking the wrong question. It is easy for me to appear and feel spiritual and loving when I'm in a spotlight, but the real me was born, lives, and continues to grow in the dark. I am discovering that my life is not a single note that I whistle to myself while I ignore the rest of the symphony of life that God would have me participate in. I have this lifetime to learn to love God. But Jesus wants me to surrender all that I am to him now, so that he can live through me. I remember the words of Dr. Frank Gripka, a spiritual mentor: "Jesus has not come to get me through this life but to live in me through it." I am not the hero of my own story, Christ is.

In recent years, some parts of life have grown more mysterious to me. In my mind I used to run through a list of solutions to life's problems even as I was listening to someone telling me about her pain and struggle. I have torn that list into little pieces.

But other fundamental answers now seem very simple. I know that Jesus loves me. I know that God is faithful. I know that he answers prayer, many times in ways I may not understand.

That is why I am writing this book. I want to invite you to sing this song with me. We may have no control over the newspaper headlines or the world's turmoil, but we can choose how we live our lives. That is not a small thing. I pray that as we make this melody together, God will speak to us. We wait for the New Jerusalem, but long before I see the sun rising on that shining city, I want to know Jesus. With all my heart and all my soul I want to know Jesus. The lessons that you learn may well be different from mine. You are writing your own story. But I invite you to join me in this symphony of the soul. I encourage you to take a little time, find out what really matters, become strong enough to be tender and wise enough to be simple. There is no greater calling in this world, of that I am sure.

If you wish to live richly, deeply and spiritually you must cultivate the "world within." It is a thrilling world with the Heavenly Father as our companion.

JOHN T. BENSON JR.,
THE NASHVILLE TENNESSEAN

PART ONE

DISCOVERY

When we enter upon the spiritual life, we should consider and examine to the bottom what we are.

BROTHER LAWRENCE,
THE PRACTICE OF THE PRESENCE OF GOD

I love large boxes. As a child on Christmas morning I was drawn to the largest parcels, despite my mother's assurance that the best gifts sometimes come in the smallest packages. There was something about the size that I wanted to celebrate. It has to be good if it's that big, I reasoned.

One birthday my brother Stephen presented me with an enormous box. I was amazed. Every year he gave me writing paper and envelopes, always pointing out what a practical gift it was: "Now you have something to write and thank me on!"

But this was different—far too big to be writing paper and envelopes. I stared at the box for a while trying to imagine what it was. I put it to one side and opened my other gifts, my gaze constantly returning to the grand prize. Finally there was nothing left but the biggest and best. I opened it carefully. Inside the large box was one a little smaller. I took it out and opened it: another box a little smaller still. Twelve boxes later I opened my pale cream writing paper and envelopes. Stephen rolled around on the carpet laughing at my surprised look. It was actually a lovely gift. It just was not what I had been looking for.

Perhaps that is a good place to begin. In understanding what *is not* we can begin to look for what *is*. I believe that I lost touch with the deepest part of my soul, my true spiritual life, because it's not what I was looking for. The things that came in large boxes with multicolored ribbons seemed so much more appealing. As a speaker and singer, public approval was very important to me. I saw new opportunities of doing bigger and better things as a sign of spiritual growth. With each passing year as the number of people at my concerts swelled and my books sold more, I knew that I had to be doing better as a Christian. More lives were being touched, I reasoned; I was more useful to God. The truth was, however, that although my box was bigger every year, if you peeled through all the layers, you'd find that I was lost under increasingly more stuff.

I used to be so sure of so many things, but I discovered that they were not much without the wrapping. It seems to me that I don't know as much as I used to. Christ's life on earth was simple: "Love God with all you have and are and love one another" (see Matthew 22:37). There is no fancy way to wrap that. It is the simple, profound truth about our lives. That is why I am here: Sheila Walsh is here on planet Earth to learn how to love God and to love her neighbor as herself. That is it. I can choose to make a huge fancy parcel and production of the whole thing, but that would miss the point. I am not the gift. I will never be the gift. Christ is the gift.

So I begin here. I lay everything else aside and I invite the Lord to show me what is true and vital. It is my heart's desire to rediscover my soul, to prepare my life to be a dwelling place for God. With God's grace I will peel away the superfluous wrapping and worship Christ, the Gift.

REAL LIFE

He has showed you, O man, what is good. And what does the LORD require of you? To act justly and to love mercy and to walk humbly with your God.

MICAH 6:8

*W*hat makes you think that you would be suited for this job, Sheila?"

I looked at the man behind the desk. He was about forty years old, beginning to lose his hair, with a goatee and rosy cheeks. "I think that I am a compassionate person, and also, as a Christian, I believe I would have a lot to offer here," I replied.

"You understand that you would not be hired as a missionary but as a housemother?" he said, a little concerned about my Christian talk.

"Oh yes, I understand that," I said. "But I believe that God would give me strength and grace to love these boys."

At the end of the week the job was mine.

I was twenty-two years old. After graduating from London Bible College, I had worked for a year in Europe with Youth for Christ as part of a one-year musical team that traveled across Europe evangelizing in schools and colleges. When my time was up, I wasn't quite sure what God wanted me to do with my life, so I began to look for a job at home, in Scotland. I saw an ad in our local paper; a school for emotionally disturbed teens was looking for a housemother. I immediately felt drawn to this position at Thornton House. In my mind I saw myself working with these boys, loving them, and helping them to find a sense of purpose for their lives.

I was to be a live-in mom to nine boys aged thirteen to sixteen. I was intimidated when I realized that most of the "boys" were taller than I and didn't immediately respond to my friendship. But I knew I would win them over. I would love them with the love of the Lord, which they would not be able to resist. I thought that until a couple of months later when they broke in to my room, hit me over the head with a bottle, and stole my jewelry.

I was so afraid. I pulled on some street clothes and ran out of the building into the woods. It was a dark, rainy night; I ran and ran till I finally fell down on the grass in tears.

I wanted so much to love these boys, but now I was afraid of them and I wanted to leave, to get as far away as possible—back to the safety of my own home.

The next morning the supervisor called me into his office. "So how are you doing?" he asked. "I guess last night was pretty scary for you."

"Yes, it was," I said. "I'm not sure I can do this."

"Would you like to read their files?"—files meant for the social workers more than for the housemothers.

He sent me off with a file on each boy. I took them out into the garden and sat under a tree. What I read was heartbreaking. Stories of sexual abuse, of battery. At thirteen, some of the boys had seen more heartache and pain than most of us will in a lifetime.

It was a very humbling experience. I had thought that I could just walk in there, be loving for a few weeks, and their lives would be transformed. How arrogant. I stayed on at Thornton House, and that yearlong experience was the beginning of some major discoveries. I discovered that I don't have enough love to mend the wounds of a broken world. I discovered that there are no quick fixes for a lifetime of pain. I discovered that the best I could do for these boys was just to be there, to listen, to pray for them, to be a friend, to be patient and kind, and to trust God to touch the broken places in their souls. It was humbling to let go of my super-Christian image, my ideas of swooping in to save the day. I had to realize that the day would probably not be saved. But if I could let God love them through me then perhaps a life would be.

A few years later I was back in my hometown with my band doing a concert. Sitting in my dressing room at the end of the evening, I heard a knock at the door. I opened it and saw a young, smartly dressed man.

"Do you remember me?" he said.

When a smile broke out across his face, I knew who he was. I'll call him Sam. He was one of the boys from my unit. "Sam, come in. It's so good to see you," I said. "How are you?"

"Just great, thanks," he said. "I prayed with you tonight; I gave my life to God."

I have heard those words many times over the years, but never have they meant as much as they did that night—coming from this boy who had been beaten by his father on weekends, who had become my friend, who stood before me now as my brother in Christ.

For me, walking humbly before God in a broken world meant giving up my desire for short-term closure on long-term pain. To these needy boys I needed to show mercy—and leave the rest to God.

Where can I begin, Lord?
The well of pain is deep,
the bruises on his face and soul
the demons in his sleep.
I lift him softly to your side
and lay him at your feet.
Pour out your oil
on battered soil
let hate and mercy meet.

Amen.

A MIRACLE
IN TWO STEPS

He took the blind man by the hand and led him out-side the village. When he had spit on the man's eyes and put his hands on him, Jesus asked, "Do you see anything?"

He looked up and said, "I see people; they look like trees walking around."

Once more Jesus put his hands on the man's eyes. Then his eyes were opened, his sight was restored, and he saw everything clearly.

MARK 8:23–25

$\mathcal{P}$ain has a way of cutting through lethargy like a flame through snow. We can spend years in spiritual apathy. Then one day our world may be shaken, and suddenly we have to respond one way or another. We can no longer remain sluggish and dull.

I strongly identify with the blind man in this story from Mark's gospel. The physical realities of his encounter with Jesus closely resemble the spiritual realities in my life. His miracle took place in two parts. The first time Jesus touched him he received a semblance of sight, enough to distinguish shapes. People looked liked trees to him. If that had been all that happened, his life would have been better than the total darkness he had lived in before he met Jesus. He could tell that the shapes were people, that they were moving around, that he was in a group. But there was more in store for him. Christ touched his eyes again and his sight was com-pletely restored. He saw people clearly. What a miracle!

I have been a Christian since I was eleven years old. That was my first life-changing encounter with Jesus. The Light of the World came into my life. As I grew up, I knew I wanted to be in touch with heaven and live in a way that would be pleasing to God. I have never doubted that the only hope for any of us is a personal relationship with God through his Son Jesus Christ and that I was called to communicate God's love. That is how I have spent my life.

But about five years ago I went through a spiritual catharsis. I had a wonderful job as co-host of a daily national religious broadcast. I enjoyed success as a writer and singer. Then my life fell apart, and I was hospitalized for clinical depression. I received treatment for this illness, and as I emerged from the other side of the tunnel, I was a different person. I saw people differently. It was as if, in the hospital, Christ had touched my eyes for a second time. Now instead of seeing shapes in front of me who needed to know God, I saw people, really saw them. It was shocking to me at first. I would look into the eyes of someone I had known for some time and see pain I had never seen there before. I would look at someone who was angry with me and see beyond the anger to a deeper hurt, and I recognized that look, that cry for help. I used to see needs and now I see people. I was so caught up in my own world of doing good things for God that I was asleep to the realities all around me.

Only the grace of God can open our eyes so that we are spiritually clear-sighted. As I read the Bible I find something that encourages me more than I can say: Christ has a heart for healing blind people. You just have to ask.

Underneath the healing flow
miracles of mercy grow.
Sight is given to the blind
washed again a second time

Wash me now, dear Lord.

Amen.

A Thankful Heart

Let the peace of Christ rule in your hearts, since as members of one body you were called to peace. And be thankful.

COLOSSIANS 3:15

*I*f I am in my car between noon and two o'clock, I listen to Dr. Laura Slessenger's radio program. People call in asking for her counsel. Some days I cringe when I hear the caller lay out a situation, because Dr. Laura's main concern is not to win popularity contests but to speak the truth, however painful that may be to hear. And at times the truth is fairly brutal.

I was driving home from a speaking engagement recently and I tuned in to her show. The woman caller was very upset at her stepmother, who had never lived up to the daughter's expectations of what a mother should be. The caller had never known her own mother, and for thirty years she had allowed herself to be wounded over and over when her new "mom" didn't measure up.

I felt real sympathy for this woman. There are so many things in life that are just not fair. Life seems random and cruel to many people.

Dr. Laura didn't appear to share my sympathy. And I was struck by her simple message that has enormous potential to impact our lives. I'm paraphrasing a little, but she said something like this:

You have a choice. You can spend your life being angry at what you did not get out of life or you can count your blessings for what you have.

We all have losses in our lives. But if we choose to feast on them every day, they numb our souls to the good with which

God has gifted us. I miss my dad. I would love to have grown up with a father. I would love to have been able to talk to him about men, to tell him when I was afraid, to have him tell me that I was beautiful, but he died when I was a child. Sometimes at school functions I would look at other fathers and wish that I was at my dad's side. I could have spent the rest of my life regretting that or blaming my poor choices or lack of courage on the fact that I lost my father, but the flip side has much more to offer. I *have* a wonderful mother, who was there for me in ways that my friends with two parents didn't always experience. I have a wonderful husband who treats me as if I were the Queen of England. My life is good.

We can choose to remain in a sleepy sluggish state regretting what is not, or we can become alive and fully awake to what is good and true about our lives.

That evening, as I took my golden retriever for a long walk, I sat looking over the ocean and reflecting on the day. I thought again that sometimes we don't notice what we have in our own backyards because it doesn't look like we think it should. I'm sure your childhood was not perfect. Maybe your loss or anger involves your dad or your husband or your wife or your stepson or yourself. Sometimes we are so aware of what is not there that we miss what we have. Yet the very act of being grateful for what we do have multiplies our gratitude and opens our eyes so that we see that we have even more than we thought we had at the start.

Can a grateful heart change our actions and our relationships? The woman who called Dr. Laura will never have the mother of her dreams, but I propose that by loving her mother and encouraging her and being the kind of daughter she herself would like to have, the caller might see the stepmom blossom. Yet even if that does not happen, it is the right thing to do, to choose to act with a grateful heart. Cultivating gratitude removes us from being *victims* to being free to love and act as we are called to do.

Paul encouraged the church at Colosse to let the peace of Christ rule in their hearts. I believe that living with a thankful heart is a large part of that process. Waking the soul is more than a one-time conversion. It is a daily turning from what is destructive to what is Christlike. If this sounds too Pollyanna-like for you, let me remind you of several things that are true for those who follow after Christ.

1. God loves you.
2. Christ has already paid for your sins.
3. Your eternal home is secure with him in heaven.
4. There will come a day when every tear will be wiped away and every heart be made new.
5. You are not alone, for Christ is with you every moment of every day.
6. You are a child of the King of kings. That is your eternal identity.

I know that life can be hard sometimes, and I encourage you to take time to grieve your losses, but do not be defined by them. Use them by the grace and strength of God as stepping-stones to a deeper life, a life of peace, a life lived with a thankful heart.

Dear Lord,
Thank you that you love me.
Thank you that my home is secure with you for eternity.
Thank you that because of you I am never alone.
Thank you.

Amen.

A NEW AND LIVING WAY

Therefore, brothers, since we have confidence to enter the Most Holy Place by the blood of Jesus, by a new and living way opened for us through the curtain, that is, his body, and since we have a great priest over the house of God, let us draw near to God with a sincere heart in full assurance of faith, having our hearts sprinkled to cleanse us from a guilty conscience and having our bodies washed with pure water.

HEBREWS 10:19–22

*I*t was the darkest night that Egypt could remember. Years later people talked in hushed tones about that night of death. Not even Pharaoh had been spared. All his power and wealth could not hold back the hand that had taken his oldest son. Some said that on a quiet night you could still hear the weeping and wailing of the mothers of Egypt as if the very ground had preserved their cries.

A group of slaves in Egypt, the children of Israel, had been warned of the coming disaster. They had been given very detailed instructions about what to do. The Lord had told Moses and Aaron,

> Tell the whole community of Israel that on the tenth day of this month each man is to take a lamb for his family, one for each household. . . . The animals you choose must be year-old males without defect, and you may take them from the sheep or the goats. . . . Then they are to take some of the blood and put it on the sides and tops of the doorframes of the houses where they eat the lambs. . . . The blood will be a sign for you on the houses where you are;

and when I see the blood, I will pass over you. No destructive plague will touch you when I strike Egypt. *Exodus 12:3, 5, 7, 13*

On that night of death not a sound came from the homes of the Israelites. Not even a dog barked. But from Egyptian homes wails rose to the sky, as mothers cradled their dead sons in their arms. As the angel of death swept over the land, only the homes with blood spread on the doorframes were spared. It is no small thing to defy God.

One of the greatest steps in discovering who we are is discovering who God is. God is a God of justice and righteousness, without guilt or sin. He is pure and holy in a way we cannot begin to grasp with our human understanding.

After Moses had been with God, his face glowed. When Isaiah saw the Lord high and lifted up, he was overwhelmed with the reality of his own sinfulness. Mortal man cannot stand before this awesome God. But in the heart of God a way had been prepared from the beginning. Desiring a relationship with his people, God gave a gift. Through Christ's sacrifice on the cross blood has been spilled on the doorframe of the hearts of every man and woman who trusts in him. We deserve the judgment of God, and we receive the mercy of God.

There will come a day that will make that night in Egypt pale in comparison. When the Lord returns there will be great joy and great sorrow. Those who have shaken their fists at God will call for the mountains to fall on them. It will be too late to change. Only those who stand covered by the blood of the Lamb will be saved.

Until that day we live our lives. We wash our cars and walk our dogs and love our children, but we live in dark days. Glance at a newspaper or turn on the six o'clock news and you can see how fast we as a nation are throwing ourselves off a cliff. But the

New Testament writer of Hebrews reminds us of who we are and where we stand. He exhorts us to draw near to God with a sincere heart in full assurance of faith, because we have been washed clean by the blood of God's perfect Lamb. Who we are in ourselves is not enough, but who we are in Christ is everything.

God the Father took his heart
and laid it at our feet,
a tiny baby thrust into our hands,
and as we pulled the carpet out beneath those
   bloodied feet
he poured forgiveness on our broken land.

Thank you, Father, Amen.

VISION

For when [King] David had served God's purpose in his own generation, he fell asleep.

ACTS 13:36

*O*ne year my summer job was working behind the haberdashery counter of the largest department store in town. It took me a while to become familiar with all the stock. We had roll upon roll of ribbon, boxes of buttons, zippers, cotton thread, pretty handkerchiefs, and one very strange item.

I came across it one day when business was slow and my boss told me to clean out all the drawers. It had obviously been some time since they had been cleaned, and I spent most of the day rerolling ribbon and putting buttons into little boxes. The item was in the bottom drawer. I pulled it out and dusted it off and thought, "What a stupid thing. No one wants one like that." I dusted it off and put it back in the drawer, convinced it would never sell.

When Miss Ferguson came back from her afternoon tea break, she asked me how my task was progressing. I showed her all the clean drawers, the neat rows of ribbon, and the boxes of buttons. I didn't mention the item in the bottom drawer. Perhaps she had ordered it. It was hardly my place to tell her that I thought it was about the stupidest thing that this sixteen-year-old had ever seen. The trouble is that I can never leave things alone. I'm like a terrier who buries a bone in the yard and digs it up every twenty minutes to see if it's still there. I couldn't contain myself.

"Miss Ferguson," I began, "we have only one of those items in the bottom drawer."

"Oh, I know," she said. "We sold so many in May and June."

You have got to be kidding! I thought.

She continued. "I'm sure we had at least twenty at the beginning of the summer. You can imagine how popular they are with our young ladies."

"You mean girls buy these?" I asked incredulously.

"Of course, dear, who else?"

"Well, I wouldn't want one," I said doggedly.

"Oh, they all say that, but someday you will," she replied with a smile.

"Miss Ferguson, I don't mean to be rude, but what would I want with a lacy plunger?"

Miss Ferguson, who was in her seventies, looked as if she were about to choke.

"A what?" she cried.

"A lacy plunger," I said. "It's not very practical and the lace will get wet when you stick it in the sink."

"My dear child," she said with tears rolling down her cheeks, "this is for bridal bouquets. You arrange the flowers in the top and you carry it by the white handle decorated with lace.

I could have died. By the next day the "lacy plunger" story was all over the store. Salespeople can be merciless!

How wrong I had been in miscalculating this item's purpose. One verse buried in the Acts of the Apostles refers to King David, who "served God's purpose in his own generation." Christ, too, was so clear in the purpose of his life. His mission statement was well defined. Do you and I know why we are here, what we have been made for, our purpose? Sometimes we live out what other people perceive as our vision and calling and never discover for ourselves what that really is. Sometimes we are afraid to reach out and live the life that we believe we have been called to. But fear is no friend. It may seem to protect, but it slowly suffocates.

Someone recently asked me if I could state in a sentence what my life is all about. I replied, "The purpose of my life is to learn to love God more and to communicate that love and grace to others." That is why I am on the planet. When you know what your mission statement is, life is so much easier; you become free to line up your activities, relationships, and goals with that stated intent. What is your place in the kingdom of God? If I were to ask you to give me a sentence that encapsulated your vision for your life, what would it be? David discovered his purpose and fulfilled it in his generation, and so must we. Otherwise, you and I could be using our lives to clean sinks, when we were made for so much more!

> *Be thou my vision, O Lord of my heart;*
> *Naught be all else to me, save that thou art:*
> *Thou my best thought, by day or by night,*
> *Waking or sleeping, thy presence my light.*
>
> ANCIENT IRISH PRAYER,
> TRANS. BY MARY BYRNE

PART TWO

THIRST

Remembering speechlessly we seek the great forgotten language, the lost lane-end into heaven, a stone, a leaf, an unfound door. Where? When?

THOMAS WOLFE,
LOOK HOMEWARD ANGEL

*T*he man and woman wandered for days on end. They were in unfamiliar territory and they were lost. They looked for anything that might point them toward home, but the landscape was barren and nameless.

"I need to rest," the woman said. "I can't walk any farther."

Her husband looked at her for a moment, a world of words behind his own tired eyes, but he said nothing and looked for a sheltering rock. They stopped, and within moments he could hear rhythmic breathing at his side; he knew she was fast asleep. He walked for a little while till he found himself on the edge of a cliff. It was a starry night, and the moon cast a long ribbon of gold across the valley. Tears poured down his face. He was alone. The pain inside was so tangible he thought it would literally tear him in two.

Why? Why? Why? The question ate at him like a cancer. Home. That reality was as distant as the moon, and yet the memory was fresh and powerful. *We will never be home again,* he thought, and it stabbed him to his very soul. He picked up a handful of earth and let the dust run through his fingers.

"We will have to make a living out of this," he said to the wind as it carried the particles away.

"Adam, Adam, where are you?"

The wind that blew away the dust brought his wife's voice back to him and he turned toward the rock.

I have often wondered what it was like for Adam and Eve after they were banished from the Garden of Eden. They lost so much. They lost intimate fellowship with God in a place of exquisite beauty and peace. They lost a simple faith and trust in each other. They lost their home. I imagine that, even as their lives moved on and family came, there was always an aching void inside, times when they would look at each other with anger or pain in their eyes and know what they had done.

Since the Fall, we all feel a similar sense of loss, and our relationships are tainted by mistrust and fear. Even in the most happy, fulfilled moments of our lives, we, like Adam and Eve, quietly long for something more. We are thirsty for a life lived beyond our legacy from the Eden exit. Before the Fall we had a perfect place on this earth, and now we do not. We long for the comforts of home—the perfect home. Jesus said, "In my Father's house are many rooms; if it were not so, I would have told you. I am going there to prepare a place for you" (John 14:2). That is our hope and our final destination. Until that day we have each other.

Here and now, the only part of eternity that we get to touch is each other. As sons and daughters of Adam and Eve, we tend to live as isolated beings, locked into the invisible walls of our mind. We need to reach beyond our fears because we need each other; right beside us is another soul who longs for home, another soul who can help us discern the signs along life's road, as they give us input and as we reach out to them.

Heaven Celebrates Our Birth

Immediately, something like scales fell from Saul's eyes, and he could see again.

ACTS 9:18

I picked up my Bible and sat on the sofa waiting for my mother and sister to change clothes. With the impatience of an eleven-year-old, I drummed my fingers on the arm of the sofa.

I was excited about this evening's concert. I had never heard a gospel group before. They were called The Heralds and they were from Edinburgh. The event was held in the local movie theater, which meant that the seats were more comfortable than church, and I hoped the candy station would be open.

But it wasn't. No smell of popcorn filled the air. *The folks who organized this event blew it!* I thought. *Christians eat a lot.*

We sat behind another family from our church. The daughter, Rosalind, was one of my best friends.

When the group was introduced, I could not take my eyes off the trombone player's red pants. It was like watching a London bus jumping around onstage. The musicians were very good, and I looked around the theater to see if any of my friends from school were there. I had invited several of my classmates who didn't go to church, and I was hoping that this evening would touch them.

After about an hour of music, a man stepped to the center mike and introduced himself as Ian Leitch. He talked about the love of God. I craned my neck to see if one particular boy in my class was "getting it," when Ian said something that made me snap back and pay attention.

"God has no grandchildren, only sons and daughters. Just because your parents go to church does not mean that you have a relationship with God by osmosis."

"What's *osmosis?*" I whispered to my mom.

"It means that you can't absorb it," she said. "You need to choose for yourself."

I was devastated. My nice little safe church world suddenly seemed like a very drafty place. As he continued, it became clear to me that I was not a Christian. I was hardly ever out of church, but I was not a Christian. I had never invited Christ into my life. I began to shake as tears rolled down my cheeks. Ian invited people to come to the stage if they wanted to surrender their lives to Christ. I couldn't move. Suddenly Rosalind got up out of her seat and walked to the front of the theater. My heart was pounding, my head was pounding, but I could not move. It was as if my legs had melted into a river, and I knew that they would not hold me up. I watched as people streamed to the front. I saw the boy from my class at school go forward and I cried even more. I thought that he needed God, but now he would be part of the family and I would not. The concert came to a close and everyone began to leave. I noticed that my mother reached over and hugged Rosalind's mother.

As we rode the bus home, Ian's words played over and over in my head. A huge struggle was going on inside me. I was afraid. The picture presented that evening had been overwhelming. It made the flannelgraphs and action choruses in Sunday school seem trivial. It was clear to me now: Being a Christian was not a hobby. It was giving God all of your life.

I got ready for bed and kissed Mom good night. I tried to sleep, but the very air around me seemed charged with the anticipation of my response. God had spoken my name and I had to reply. I got out of bed and went back downstairs. "Mom, can you give your life to Christ only in a meeting, or would it be possible at home?"

My mother reassured me that God listens to our prayers wherever we are. So that evening, when I was eleven years old, as my mother prayed with me and led me to the door of the kingdom, my life changed forever. I was young, but I understood clearly that this was the most important thing that would ever happen to me, even if I lived to be a hundred. I lay awake for hours, feeling more alive than ever. I had no idea what my life would be like, but I knew that it would be forever.

The Holy Spirit may have moved differently in your life. For some it is a slow process of coming to faith; for others it is a sudden confrontation on the road. But for all of us—when we are called from death to life, when we discover what we were really made for, heaven celebrates our birth.

> *Behind the things we see and feel,*
> *beyond the reach of what seems real,*
> *a deeper thirst calls us by name;*
> *and turning to that sweet refrain,*
> *our eyes behold you, Lamb of God,*
> *and running now o'er well-worn sod we quench our thirst*
>   *in Thee.*
>
> *Amen.*

Soul to Soul

Be merciful to me, O LORD, for I am in distress;
my eyes grow weak with sorrow, my soul and my body
with grief.

PSALM 31:9

*I*t was a breezeless day with the hot sun beating down on the
sticky Tarmac. I had accepted an invitation to sing in a women's
prison in Texas and the band was setting up on the blacktop. A
few women gathered around, lighting up their cigarettes and
making suggestive comments. I thought that they were directed
toward the guys in the band; then the warden informed me that
I was the topic of their conversation. The warden had brought
in some additional security from the male prison a few miles
away. Stepping to the mike, it was hard to ignore the guards with
guns. They looked particularly sour because they had to stand
out in the blazing sun listening to a Scottish Pollyanna sing about
God's love.

I looked into the eyes of these incarcerated women as I sang
and I wondered if anything I had to say came close to touching
the world they lived in. The warden had filled me in on some of
their backgrounds and the crimes that had brought them behind
these walls. Murder, manslaughter, and child abuse. I knew nothing of this world. They stared back at me as if I were from a
mythical planet where life was as you'd always hoped it could be
as a child. *How can I reach them?* I wondered.

Then I had an idea. I asked my lead guitarist, a mean
blues player, to take the stage. As he allowed his instrument to
sing out the song of the lost and lonely, I saw the women draw
close. "Amen, brother," someone shouted, as she swayed to the

heartbreaking melody that filled the air. There were no words, but no words were needed. Words would have been a hindrance because every story was different—but every heart, every soul, was the same.

I sat on the edge of the stage, captivated by the music and the women's faces as tears poured down their cheeks. There was a connection. It was soul to soul. The melody flowed behind the anger, the fear, and the defenses of us all, and it witnessed to the ache to be loved and accepted. For a moment it was as if the rain from heaven quenched the thirst in all of us to be heard, to be seen. I will never forget that day. I saw that beyond the choices that we make for our lives, some good and some that lead us down the path of destruction, there is a common bond. It is our eternal nature, our soul.

So what is the soul? It is the deepest aspect of ourselves, the spiritual part that cries out for heaven, that is made to be a dwelling place for God. Nothing and no one else can answer that thirst. It is the size of eternity.

> *The longing filled the room.*
> *It hung in the sticky air like a fly caught in a paper trap*
> *suspended in its frailty.*
> *Our thirst was for you.*
> *It was for you we wept.*
> *For a moment all walls came down*
> *all voices were stilled*
> *As God in Christ walked prison halls and spoke to us*
>   *by name.*
> *Thank you.*
>
> *Amen.*

WHEN YOU'VE LOST YOUR THIRST

I will pour water on him who is thirsty.

ISAIAH 44:3 NKJV

I usually take care of my car, but a few months ago I was so busy training our new golden retriever puppy and doing some library research that I ignored the odometer that indicated an oil change was, well, overdue. My car seemed to be fine and I promised myself that I would do it "next week."

Then when I was pumping gas one day, an eager attendant asked if he could check my oil. He disappeared under the hood, and when he reappeared, he gazed at me as if I were a child molester. He held up a rod, black with sticky gunk.

I got the message, and the next day I dropped my car off for an oil change. When I picked it up, I could not believe the difference. It was as if I was driving a new vehicle. I had become so used to its sluggish behavior that I had forgotten how well my car can perform—if it's taken care of.

I see my soul as being like my car. As a vehicle needs clean oil, I need intimate contact with God. Our souls were made for this. When we deprive our souls of that very life force, we can survive—but that is all we are doing. We were not created to merely survive but to thrive in God.

This is a constant struggle for me. I am very headstrong and independent. Even though I know I need that intimate communion that settles my soul, I still run on blindly at times, not willing to stop and get the refreshment that would revitalize my whole being.

Sometimes we know we need refreshment but are too lazy in the routine of life—or too preoccupied with what we think is "important"—to stop for spiritual replenishment. Sometimes life may crowd in on us enough that we simply are not aware of our need. Think of the need for intimacy with God in terms of physical thirst. In the routine demands and distractions of the day, we can forget this most basic of all needs. I notice that on a hot day my dog, Bentley, is always returning to his water bowl for a drink. We might be playing with his ball, but at regular intervals he heads off for more water. Sometimes it's only in watching him that I realize how thirsty I am; I have the beginnings of a headache caused by dehydration. It's not wise to wait to change the oil when your car is running on treacle. It's not wise to wait to drink a glass of water after the headache is so bad you have to go and lie down in a dark room.

It is the same in our relationship with God. We can run through our days ignoring our need for him—intentionally or unintentionally—until we find ourselves dry and worn out.

If you sense you have lost touch with a thirst for God, talk to him about it. There is no glory in pretending and no shame in admitting what is true. Start with an honest confession to God that you have been distracted or negligent. Thank him for reminding you of your need—your thirst. We have forgotten how well we were meant to run.

> *Create in me a thirst, Lord,*
> *that only you can fill.*
> *Take this broken fragile life*
> *this stubborn selfish will.*
> *Renew in me a thirst for you.*
> *My heart is dry and cold.*
> *Break through the earth, a spirit birth.*
> *Dear Lord, restore my soul.*

A THIRST
FOR COMMUNITY

Now you are the body of Christ, and each one of you is a part of it.

1 CORINTHIANS 12:27

When the Church wakes again it will know that there can be no consequential change in the lives of people unless there is community.

ELIZABETH O'CONNOR,
OUR MANY SELVES

I have always viewed the psalms as intimate deeply personal prayers and songs. But it seems the psalms were liturgical poems used for corporate worship. They were read and sung aloud as a statement of faith of the people of God.

That communal purpose points out the huge obsession we in American Christianity have with self-discovery. In communal worship there is an accountability that does not allow us voyeuristically to point a finger at the world or the church; communal worship says we are part of the problem and are called to be part of the solution. That is one of the reasons I would like to live in a small town.

It seems to me that as a Christian this is all I need in life as I walk with God: a small group of people to live alongside, to learn from, to disagree with, to be changed by.

I used to love big cities and big malls, but I think maybe really I liked the anonymity of being able to disappear in such a setting and be accountable to no one. I cannot change on my own. I have tried and it doesn't work. I need to rub up against others to have my rough edges soothed away.

Last night Barry and I went to see a movie with friends—*The Spitfire Grill*. What I loved about it was the accountability of small-town life. Everyone knew each other, and the events of every family touched everyone else.

The town in the movie was called Gilead. The meaning was clear. There is a balm in Gilead. There is healing in community. The town was full of characters, the nosy postmistress, the insecure judgmental husband, the intimidated wife, the broken Vietnam veteran. The townsfolk frequently clashed, but on one level that was good news, because in that process they were forced to look at themselves; in that process they were given an opportunity to change. If that husband and wife, for example, had lived in a big city where their relationship was hidden behind high walls of anonymity, I'm sure they eventually would have become a divorce statistic. If the war veteran had lived in a heartless city, he would have slipped into obscurity, one more bum to give a wide berth to on the street corner. But they all lived in a the cauldron of a little town that caused them to be seen as they really were.

That is what the church is supposed to be like. So often these days we hide within the walls of large churches. We come in as strangers and we leave the same way. We smile at one another, give the impression that we are the one family that has it all together, and go home to our private wars. Life was not meant to be that cold. We need each other so badly. Respectability is a thin coat on a winter's day. It is better to be known with all our hypocrisy and failings. We are the body of Christ, and deep inside each of us is a thirst to be known and loved, to be part of the stream of life. As we sing the psalms together, we see ourselves and each other and yet we see our frailties within the context of the grace and mercy of God.

We can't all pack up and head for some mythical town in Maine, hoping that within the space of a two-hour movie our lives will have taken on more meaning. But we can all begin to change how we live. We can start a small group in our home where we commit to grow together. We can be more real and present in our families. We can take our eyes off ourselves and our own journey and realize that this is a group outing—that we are not supposed to arrive in heaven alone but hand in hand.

> *Called to love with hearts as strong and deep as rivers run,*
> *Called to live beyond ourselves, beyond the webs*
>   *we've spun,*
> *Called to laugh with those who laugh, to cry, to weep,*
>   *to sing,*
> *to give ourselves, to live an offering.*
>
> *Amen.*

WAIT FOR GOD

What can a man give in exchange for his soul?
MARK 8:37

*A*ll human love bears within it the seed of betrayal; it is a failure of love. No one knows that more than Judas Iscariot, that notorious betrayer who was quickly overwhelmed by the horror of his dastardly deed—but his remorse receives little press. Here's the Gospel account:

> When Judas, who had betrayed him, saw that Jesus was condemned, he was seized with remorse and returned the thirty silver coins to the chief priests and the elders. "I have sinned," he said, "for I have betrayed innocent blood."
> *Matthew 27:3–4*

What lay under that act of betrayal? Perhaps a deep thirst to right all wrongs now, to grasp hold of justice with his own two hands and pull it into his world. I see Judas's life as one that spoke of impatience. I see a deep thirst for more than the life he had lived as a young man. I imagine him leaving his father's vineyards in Kerioth, frustrated and restless; this farm life was not for him. There had to be more. He wanted Christ to act in ways that made sense to him. He wanted a savior of his own molding. Deep within his soul he was thirsty for a different life, but he wasn't willing to wait for the "something more" Christ would offer.

Even in the end, after the betrayal, Judas could not hold on. Now he stood with the rope in his hands, clenching the tool that would end his miserable life. His heart thundered in his ears, his stomach retched. What a fool he had been. His mind treated him to a picture show of a thousand memories that had brought him to this moment. He thought of his father, of boyhood friends, but he felt he couldn't go to them; none of them would understand what he had done. He had no choice but to end a life that had tipped the first domino for someone else. He could not bear to think of Jesus now. He could not bring himself to watch what he had participated in. He threw the rope over a sturdy branch.

But if he had waited three more days he would have seen Christ risen from the dead.

When we abandon ourselves to hopelessness we remove ourselves from Christ, our only hope—like the lemmings, who hurl themselves from a cliff into the sea. If only Judas could have held on a little longer. As Ray Anderson writes in his book on the life of Judas: "At the same moment that Judas is enacting the human drama of sin and death, Jesus is enacting the divine drama of redemption and atonement."

Augustine said that our hearts are restless until they rest in God, but we try all sorts of things to still that pounding in our heads and the ache in our souls. For some, it is the promise of success and what that golden cloak will feel like. For others it is the frantic, futile search for that one person who will fully understand us and make us whole. For Judas? Perhaps a chip on his shoulder and a desire for power that would make him feel like he was someone to reckon with.

There is no doubt that what he did was the ultimate act of betrayal, but I think of the words of Jesus on the cross: "Father, forgive them, for they do not know what they are doing" (Luke 23:34). I wonder if Judas was one of the people on his mind.

Our impatience to have God move now, to act in ways that make sense to us, will drive us to take control of our lives. God is moving in ways that we cannot see or understand. This means we are left with the question, "Do I trust him?" We can choose to bow the knee now and ask him to forgive us for trying to squeeze the answer we want out of heaven, or we will bow the knee later in remorse at our foolishness in thinking that we knew better than God.

We are all thirsty in different ways, deep down in our souls. It is a thirst as ancient as the hills. But it is a thirst that can be satisfied only in Christ.

Lord,
Forgive us for our impatience.
In our restlessness give us peace.
In our impatience give us hope.
In our thirst for you refresh us, we pray.

Amen.

PART THREE

PROMISES

Oh, how great peace and quietness would he possess who should cut off all vain anxiety and place all his confidence in God.

THOMAS À KEMPIS

I decided to take the Pacific Coast Highway to the radio interview in Huntington Beach. The drive along the ocean takes a little longer, but it is so much nicer than the freeway. So I left early and drove at tourist pace along the beautiful shoreline to Warren Duffy's studio. Duffy's live daily radio talk show is broadcast across the country, and he is one of my favorite interviewers. He asks the kind of questions that you have to think about before you answer. He has an Irishman's humor and quick wit.

I was his guest—to talk about my book *Honestly.* We talked about the number of Christians who struggle with clinical depression, about how hard it seems to be for us to be transparent about our lives, to admit that we have a problem. At the end of the hour Duffy asked me if I had any last thing to say that might be an encouragement to his audience.

The words that came from my heart were simple: "God is faithful."

I used to have an answer for most problems in life. I had a lot to say on almost any subject. I now have fewer answers, and they might be reduced to the simple phrase, God is faithful. I don't say that lightly or without thought; I say it because I know it is true, and I have discovered that it is true no matter what is happening in my life. With confidence, I add these words to the end of the worst statements in the world: My child is sick and I don't know what to do . . . but God is faithful; I lost my job and I don't know how I will pay my bills . . . but God is faithful; my husband has left me and my heart is torn in two . . . but God is faithful.

I don't mean that he will wave a magic wand and everything will fall into place; far from it. What I mean is that if in the darkest times in our lives we will learn to keep turning our face toward him, he is faithful. Faithful to be with us, faithful to watch over us, faithful to work in us to make us the men and women we are called to be.

Sometimes God does not *seem* to be faithful, because he doesn't answer our prayers as we expected him to. I have changed my expectations. If the whole purpose of my life is to learn to love God and to show his compassion to the world, then what he is doing *in* me is more important than what he is doing *for* me. I have discovered through many tears that if I will bring every jagged edge of my life to him, he will continue to mold me to become the woman I am called to be.

I received a lot of mail after that particular interview. People poured out their stories of hardship and trouble, but to the very last letter they said, "Thank you for reminding me of what is true. God is indeed faithful." I was so encouraged as I read each letter. My faith was built up by the testimony of others who defy all that the world has to say about what makes a human soul happy.

Whatever is happening with you right now, as your sister in Christ, I urge you to meditate on these words of life: GOD IS FAITHFUL.

And if you have time . . . take the coast road.

NEVER ALONE

The LORD himself goes before you and will be with you; he will never leave you nor forsake you. Do not be afraid; do not be discouraged.

DEUTERONOMY 31:8

I was in Bangkok, preparing for an evening concert at the largest university in the city. I was the guest of Youth with a Mission and Campus Crusade. My friends from YWAM, Steve and Marie Goode, told me this was the first time they had been able to organize a concert within these hallowed walls, and they were excited about what God would do.

"Tonight is a first," Steve said. "Bangkok is a hard city to penetrate spiritually. The people are very religious, but much of their religion is based on fear."

I thought of all the little houses, like dollhouses, that I saw suspended outside restaurants and stores and asked him about those. "Those are spirit houses," he told me. "The people believe that if they build a home for the evil spirits to live in, then the spirits will not come and live in the people themselves."

"How awful to live in such fear and uncertainty," I said.

Steve told me that he anticipated a lot of spiritual warfare and trouble during the concert but that there would be a continuous prayer meeting all evening. I naively thought he was being overly dramatic; after all it was just a concert. I was used to being in Britain or America where there is a certain receptivity to the Gospel, where years of prayer have soaked the soil. But in Thailand, Buddhism held sway.

As I stood at the microphone for a sound check before they opened the doors, I heard a strange scraping noise and turned to my right just in time to see a large heavy "tree" of stage lights come crashing down. I jumped out of the way as they smashed on the floor right where I had been standing. I couldn't believe it. No one had been near them to jar or bump them. There was no wind in the building. For the first time that night, I began to take Steve's words to heart.

I was delighted that a large crowd of students came. (The advertisements said that I was a pop singer from London, and British music was very popular in Bangkok.)

Before the concert began, Steve said, "We will be right behind you, just behind the curtain. We will be lifting you up in prayer every moment. God loves these students and it's time that they heard about that."

I was a little nervous, but as we prayed together before we went onstage, someone read these words: "The LORD himself goes before you and will be with you; he will never leave you nor forsake you. Do not be afraid; do not be discouraged." And for the next two hours I had to cling to that promise.

Halfway through the first song, the sound system went off and the second set of stage lights failed. There I was, standing in the dark, with no amplification. But my sponsoring team seemed prepared to jump any hurdle. I ended up singing through a bullhorn with a flashlight lighting up my face!

The amazing thing was what God did that night. Out of perhaps three thousand students more than half stayed behind to hear more about Jesus. And it certainly wasn't because they were impressed with the pop singer from London!

God is faithful to his Word. There are promises that he gives us that are surer than the blood that runs in our veins. When God says "never" it means never, not ever. We may find ourselves in places or circumstances that some would call "God-

forsaken," but when we are there with him, he is there with us.
That is a promise!

> *In the darkest place on earth he is there.*
> *Where no other shadows rest he is there.*
> *If you fall and bruise your heart,*
> *Just remember this one part,*
> *He is there.*
> *He is there.*
> *He is there.*
>
> *Amen.*

THE NEXT STEP

In all my prayers for all of you, I always pray with joy because of your partnership in the gospel from the first day until now, being confident of this, that he who began a good work in you will carry it on to completion until the day of Christ Jesus.

PHILIPPIANS 1:4

*H*ow much farther is it?" Weary asked her traveling companion.

"It's just over that hill," replied Courage.

"But we've been that way before!"

"No. Some of the hills look alike, but we haven't been here before," Courage said.

Weary looked out over the horizon and was sure that Courage was wrong. Weary recognized the slope of the hill, the trees.

"I need to sit down for a while," she said. "I'm so tired."

They sat under the shade of a large oak tree and Weary closed her eyes. In a few moments she was asleep. In her dream she saw herself at the top of a large mountain. The view was spectacular. The sky azure blue. The soft grass felt like down feathers. She heard music so breathtaking that she felt as if she were being lifted by waves of voices that swept over her and wrapped her in swaying robes. Perfect peace. She had never experienced anything like it. She knew that she wanted to stay there forever. Following the sound of the music, Weary soon saw a crowd of people singing at the other side of the mountain. She walked toward them. The crowd seemed to stretch for miles, but the harmony that came from the music was like one voice, gently layered. It was perfect. She heard a sound behind her, and as she turned, she awoke and found herself against the oak tree.

"We need to move on," Courage said.

"I just had a dream, Courage. It was the most wonderful dream I've ever had."

"Tell me about it."

"Well, I was on a mountain, but everything was so beautiful, so clear. And the singing! It took my breath away," Weary said.

"Yes, I have been there," replied Courage. "It is the most beautiful place of all."

"How do we get there?" Weary asked. "How far is it?"

"It's a long way," her companion replied.

"But I'll never make it!" she cried. "I'm too tired. I wasn't made for this."

Courage looked at her for a moment and said, "This *is* what you were made for, Weary. You just have to take the next step."

That is how I view our spiritual journey, just taking the next step. I find that hard. I want to know the whole game plan. I want to know what roads I will be on, where they will take me, how long it will take, and when it will all happen. But as a follower of Christ, all I am called to do is to take the next step.

Some of the steps are confusing to me. They don't look as if they are leading forward, and I get frustrated and impatient. When that happens I have to remind myself of two things: God is in control, and he has promised to complete the work he began in me. He may not do that in ways that make sense to me, but I have his promise that what he began, he will finish. All I have to do is to take the next step. The path may not look familiar, but it's the road home.

Lord,
When the road ahead is dark, be my light.
When the path is rough and stony, be my guide.
When the wind is fierce and in my face,
When the world is such a barren place,
Lead me on.
Lead me on.
Lead me on.

Amen.

NEVER MORE
THAN YOU CAN BEAR

No temptation has seized you except what is common to man. And God is faithful; he will not let you be tempted beyond what you can bear. But when you are tempted, he will also provide a way out so that you can stand up under it.

1 CORINTHIANS 10:13

*A*s Christians one of the greatest temptations we face is to quit. As I travel and meet people all over the country I hear more tales of discouragement than of blatant sin. Perhaps it is the legacy of some teaching that was popular in the seventies and eighties, when we were told that God wanted us to be healthy, wealthy, and wise. If we just had enough faith, a Mercedes would be parked in our driveway, our loving children would be serving God in perfect obedience, and any physical sickness would be a thing of the past. It sounded so wonderful.

I remember a discussion with a dear friend who had embraced this teaching wholeheartedly. I asked him how he would spiritually respond if one of his three lively daughters fell off a swing and broke her leg. He felt that if he had enough faith, his daughter would not fall off a swing. We talked long into the night about what faith really is. We parted as friends, but we were miles apart in our views. I soon moved away, and we didn't see each other for several years. Then we met again, both of us ministering at the same conference. I asked after the children, knowing that their lives would have moved on by leaps and bounds. Over a cup of coffee he told me about the changes in their lives.

"I thought it was going to break her mother's heart," he began. "I just wanted to kill the guy! I couldn't believe that my little girl was pregnant."

I listened as he told me about the cold wind that had blown through their home. The pregnant daughter wanted to be with the father of her child, and my friend and his wife were so against it. Great barriers developed in the family as they all retreated to their separate corners to cope with this crisis.

"All my nice neat theories went out the window," he said. "I thought I had it all tied up. I thought I understood God, but I was wrong."

"So what happened?" I asked him.

"For a while I couldn't pray," he said. "I could hardly talk to my wife or my children. I just wanted to give up. Nothing made sense to me anymore."

"But you're here today," I said. "I've just heard you sing, and I noticed a depth and a tenderness that were never there before."

"Well," he continued, "I came to the end of myself, which was very hard for me. I was a proud man, but I had to throw myself on God and tell him I couldn't take any more. And then he slowly began to rebuild me. It felt as if I were starting all over. All I knew was that Jesus loved me and he loved my wife and he loved my daughter and he loved the baby and, most difficult of all, he loved the baby's father. Just when it seemed that this thing would destroy us all, God stepped in."

It's hard to let go of things in which we have placed our hope—even when they lie broken in our hands. It's even harder to let go of our preconceived ideas of how God works when those lie shattered at our feet.

Many of us carry around a heavy weight of discouragement. It seems as if nothing will ever get any better, nothing will change. In the midst of that I offer these words of hope, of promise: "God is faithful; he will not let you be tempted beyond what you can bear."

Perhaps it seems to you that you are at the breaking point. I urge you in the name of the Lord to throw yourself on him, to hide yourself under his wings. Don't give up. You have come too far. The road ahead may look bleak, but trust in God. It is the way home.

Dear Lord,
I bring myself before you now.
I lay this discouragement at your feet.
I lay the broken pieces of my plans before you.
I rest in you.

Amen.

UNEXPECTED GIFTS

As it is written: "He has scattered abroad his gifts to the poor; his righteousness endures forever."

2 CORINTHIANS 9:9

I am pregnant! Even as I write it, I can't believe it. I look at my face in the mirror to see if I look any different. Do I look like a mother? No, I just look like me. I feel as if I could run and skip and dance, and yet at the same time I am overwhelmed with uncertainty. Will I be a good mother? I know that Barry will be a wonderful dad, but what about me? I can care for a dog and a cat, but what about a little innocent person who will need me every moment? I grab hold of myself and sit down with a cup of tea. (Can I still have tea?)

"Well, Lord, you are full of surprises!" I say. "You have known all along that this would be the moment, so I trust you to help me. Thank you for an unexpected gift."

How will I tell my husband? Tonight we are meeting our best friends, Frank and Marlene, for dinner; I am meeting Barry there. I can't tell him with other people around. I can't tell him over the phone. Oh, I hope I don't burst into tears. What shall I say to him? There is nothing in this world that will make him happier than knowing he is going to be a dad.

I think of my mom. I can't wait to call her tomorrow. She will be so happy. I think of Barry's parents. He is an only child so they will be on their knees for weeks, thanking God!

I think back over the last few years and wonder at the grace and kindness of God to me. I think of the darkest days, when it seemed as if I would never be happy or at peace again, and now I find myself the home for this precious gift from God.

That is the most poignant thought to me at the moment. There are some parts of our journey that are so dark and the terrain so bleak that it's hard to find the will to keep on walking. That is why we are called to walk by faith. We hold on to the promises of God not because they seem likely, for at times they don't, but because they come from God and it is not possible for him to lie. I pulled out an old diary the other day and read a verse that I wrote down when it was the last thing that I felt to be true about my life. "I am still confident of this: I will see the goodness of the LORD in the land of the living" (Psalm 27:13).

Today, as I allowed the doctor's words to sink in and I thought of my wonderful husband and this child whom we will be privileged to love and care for, I found myself worshiping God—who brings treasures out of the deepest caves and flowers out of the most arid soil.

> *Dear Lord,*
> *You are full of surprises.*
> *From the darkest night*
> *comes the most breathtaking sunrise.*
> *From the most unforgiving rain*
> *comes the sweetest refreshment.*
> *Thank you for unexpected gifts.*
>
> *Amen.*

THE PROMISE OF JOY

In my Father's house are many rooms; if it were not so, I would have told you. I am going there to prepare a place for you. And if I go and prepare a place for you, I will come back and take you to be with me that you also may be where I am.

JOHN 14:2–3

This is the best promise of all! I can't even imagine what that day will be like when we are finally home with Jesus. As a child I would think about heaven and worry about boredom. I imagined us all standing around the throne; after the two-thousandth round of *Kum Ba Ya,* I knew I would be twiddling my thumbs. But it won't be like that. With our human minds, there is no way we can begin to take in the joy of heaven. Our best earthly moments are pale shadows of what the rest of our eternal lives will be.

All evil will be gone; all worry, all sickness, all jealousy and anger will be so far removed from the reality of heaven that we will remember them no more. There we will live life as it was always meant to be.

Jesus made this promise to his friends—of a "prepared place" in his Father's house—before the horror of Golgotha, before the empty tomb, before the ascension to his Father's side. His words must have sounded strange to them.

"What does he mean, 'he's going away'? Where is he going and why aren't we going with him?"

But Jesus was preparing his friends for what lay ahead: "I have told you now before it happens, so that when it does happen you will believe" (John 14:29).

In the next few days these men were rocked to their foundations. They watched the cruel execution of the One in whom they had placed their hopes. They all expected something of Christ, but none had expected this.

But night turned to morning and the tomb was empty and the tortured body gone. Did Jesus' words then come back to mind? Or later, when they huddled together in a room, afraid of what might happen, disillusioned and lost, and suddenly Christ appeared among them, uttering words of peace? Or maybe they remembered when Jesus was taken from them into the clouds and the angel asked why they were standing looking into the sky. Or was it at Pentecost as the Holy Spirit fell upon them as Jesus had promised? They were changed men from that day onward. Most of the disciples were eventually martyred for their faith, but each was confident of his eternal destination—the promised home.

Sometimes it's hard in the mundane routine of our lives to keep this picture before us, and yet it is the reality that makes all the rest of our lives make sense. We have this promise to hold on to: Christ has gone before us to prepare a place for us. And, best of all, he is coming back to take us home.

When Christ shall come
With shouts of acclamation and take me home
What joy shall fill my heart.
Then I shall bow in humble adoration
And there proclaim, my God, how great Thou art.
STUART K. HINE

PART FOUR
FRIENDSHIP

Jean Valjean, my brother, you no longer belong to evil: but to good. It is your soul I am buying for you. I withdraw it from dark thoughts and from the spirit of perdition and I give it to God.

VICTOR HUGO,
LES MISERABLES

*T*he lights went up in the theater and the crowd moved toward the exits, talking, making supper plans. But I sat in silence. Tears streaming down my cheeks, I was incapable of speech. I sat for about fifteen minutes and then left, one of the few remaining stragglers.

Feeling as if I were carrying a very precious gift in my pocket, I walked through the New York theater district. I was deeply moved by this musical rendition and abridgment of Victor Hugo's marvelous work, *Les Miserables*. I kept thinking to myself, "How important one life is. One person *can* make such a difference."

In Hugo's book the central character, Jean Valjean, was released from prison after serving nineteen years—for stealing a loaf of bread. At this point Jean was no longer a man; he was a number: 24601. And his soul had been buried under the filth and inhumanity of years of torture. That first night out he walked the streets in vain, looking for a place to lay his head and for a drink of water. Kindly Bishop Myriel took him in for the night and treated him with grace and kindness. But in an attempt to survive, Jean stole the church's silver candlesticks. Quickly arrested, he was dragged through the night back to the church and thrown before the bishop. Jean's destiny hung in the balance.

In an act of Christlike grace, the bishop told the authorities that he had *given* the candlesticks to his guest. As Jean Valjean turned to leave, the bishop whispered, "Jean Valjean, my brother, you no longer belong to evil: but to good. It is your soul I am buying for you. I withdraw it from dark thoughts and from the spirit of perdition and I give it to God." This act of supreme mercy changed Valjean's life forever.

Some people might question the morality of the bishop's gift and his statement to the police. Surely this was church property used in the worship of God. Who could tell what a petty thief would do with such a treasure? But the bishop lived beyond the property of the church and saw the restorative mission of the church. He covered the sin of a stranger and offered a stranger a new beginning. There is something very powerful about having someone believing in you, someone giving you another chance.

I took a long walk today with Bentley, my golden retriever. We walked for miles over the hills, stopping at a point where we could look down on the ocean. The sun was shining and we had the place to ourselves. I like it that way because then I can sing "Great Is Thy Faithfulness" at the top of my lungs. As I watched Bentley trying to catch a lizard, I thought, *How very rich I am. I have a wonderful family—a mother, sister, and brother, and their families—whom I love and who love me. I have a husband who is kind and strong and fun. I have three friends who know me inside and out. I don't always like it when they speak the truth to me, but I treasure these relationships as if they were the Crown Jewels of England.*

If the whole purpose of our lives is to become more like Christ, and I believe it is, then we need real soul friendships in that process. It is easy to look good on the outside, to gift wrap our lives, but if the box is empty, how miserable we really are. It is easy to treat each other as we deserve, but how wonderful to treat each other as we have been treated by God, to give and give when no gift is called for.

Take a risk. Open up your heart. Find a real friend and grow together. Be a real friend and see what happens. I have experienced that kind of love from others, and I stand with Jean Valjean to tell you it is life-changing.

I Almost
Missed the Miracle

He answered: "'Love the Lord your God with all your
heart and with all your soul and with all your strength and
with all your mind'; and, 'Love your neighbor as yourself.'"
LUKE 10:27

*W*hen I was seventeen years old, I worked for part of a summer at Hansel Village, a home for mentally and physically handicapped adults. My first morning of work I was nervous as I got
off the bus and walked to the main house. I had never spent time
with anyone disabled, and I didn't know how I would react to
the residents or they to me. At lunch the matron introduced me
to the community, explaining that I would be helping out for a
few weeks. A young woman with Down's syndrome immediately
walked up to me, put her arms around me, and gave me a bear
hug. The others took her cue. I stood there for about ten minutes as, one after another, they approached and hugged me. It
was overwhelming. During my stay there I encountered a different kind of love than I had known before. It was childlike and
pure. It was freely given and based on nothing but a shared joy
and love of life. At night I would bring out my guitar and we
would sing for an hour. One or two of the men would sit at my
feet and my bear-hug friend would lay her head on my lap.

I remember one day in particular. We set off early for a
nature walk and picnic lunch. Elizabeth, one of the residents,
walked through the woods with her head down, looking at the

ground. Afraid she would bump into a tree, I asked her what she was doing.

"I'm looking for a flower," she said.

Our path was strewn with wildflowers, so I figured she was looking for one particular flower. When I asked, she told me the name of it and what it looked like. She invited me to join the search.

"You'll never find it!" one of the young men cried. "She's been looking for it for months."

After lunch most of us caught a nap, lying on the grass or leaning against the trunk of an oak tree. But not Elizabeth; her search continued. When it was time to head home, we gathered up our belongings. Just then Elizabeth came running, skipping, and dancing toward me. "I found it! I found it! I found it!" she cried, joy splashed across her face as she held the tiny bloom in her hand.

Later that evening when all the residents were asleep I wandered up to my room. There on my pillow was Elizabeth's flower—the fruit of her long search—with a short note. "To Aunt Sheila with love, your friend for always, Elizabeth."

I carry that memory and those faces with me to this day.

This is what the church is supposed to look like. How can we love God with everything and our neighbor as ourselves if we do not sacrificially give of ourselves with joy? In looking for the big opportunities to "perform" as a Christian, how many small God-given opportunities to love with depth do we miss? How many small gifts are given to us that we don't even notice—because we're waiting for the big gestures?

This year I am asking myself a new set of soulful questions:

"Do I love God more this year than last?"

"Am I more compassionate and tender?"

"Am I allowing others into my life?"

"Is the fruit of the Spirit growing in me?"

"Am I taking risks for Jesus?"

Jesus' twofold commandment to love God and others as ourselves calls for a depth of love that I do not yet know. But in the midst of my discouragement there is a strong candle burning. I have more real friends now than I have ever had. We speak the truth to each other and keep walking together. These vital life lessons cannot be learned in obscurity and isolation. They are learned in community as we are forced to face ourselves as we really are and love enough to want to change. Life lived on the edge is tough and yet full of joy. I hold those Hansel Village summer memories as some of the richest of my life. For a few weeks I found friendship and acceptance based simply on the fact that I was a fellow human being. The residents of the community did not care what I would "make" of my life, they didn't think about "grand opportunities," they simply handed out the love of God, trusting that I would receive it and give it back in return.

I almost missed the miracle.
I tried to hurry by.
Wrapped up in an old box,
unappealing to the eye,
deep inside that package
what a true gift I was given
for some of God's most broken ones
are very close to heaven.

Thank you, Lord. Amen.

A GIFT TO EACH OTHER

Therefore encourage one another and build each other up, just as in fact you are doing.

1 THESSALONIANS 5:11

*T*he small plane began its descent into Sheridan, Wyoming. My eyes drank in the scenery, green fields and mountains for as far as the eye could see. It was only September and yet some of the taller peaks were already dusted with snow. It was beautiful. At the airport Barry and I were met by Bob Phillips, pastor of the church at which I was to sing and speak the next day.

"Would you like 'the tour'?" he asked.

"Absolutely!" we replied in unison. As we rode down Main Street I expected Andy Griffith and Barney Fife to wave from the door of the old mercantile store. Out in the countryside we saw fields of antelope and deer and beautiful horses. Parts of the scene reminded me of Scotland: little brooks and streams running over stones and winding through the fields.

An hour later we pulled into the driveway of the ranch where we would be staying. They showed us to our room and we had a little time to relax before dinner. That evening was one of the most memorable of my life. Eight of us—Bob and his wife; the copastor and his wife; our hosts, Joe and Karalyn Schuchert; Barry and I—sat for hours and talked about the things that God was teaching us. It was a testimony time—but much more; I felt as if I were on holy ground. Each person spoke out of a deep love for and devotion to Christ, relating inspiring stories of how God had worked in his or her life.

As I lay in bed that night I knew that my faith had been built up by brothers and sisters who were all heading in the same direction.

"This has been one of the most amazing evenings," Barry said. "What a way to spend time together, when you all walk away richer for the experience."

As we left our hosts the next day, Karalyn expressed a similar view, adding a new insight about God's timing: "I lay in bed last night and asked God what he was doing with us all. Joe and I were supposed to be in China; we weren't even supposed to be here." She continued, "One word came to me: *refreshed.* God was refreshing us by bringing us together with each other and with him."

Yes, we all left refreshed. Even though Barry and I had traveled for five hours to get to Wyoming, we left with new hope, a new commitment to following Christ. In the company of new friends, we discovered a renewed and a profound gratitude to God for his faithfulness and a deeper desire to know him more.

We are called and privileged to bring refreshment to one another. There is so much discouragement in the world, but we as God's people can redeem the time we have with one another so that when we take our leave we are built up in Christ.

I encourage you to bring more than French bread or a lovely dessert to dinner; bring your whole self and ask God to allow you to be a source of refreshment to those around you.

> *Words of wisdom,*
> *words of blessing*
> *spilling light into the darkness.*
> *Hold the truth above the sadness,*
> *singing now with hearts of gladness,*
> *he has met us here.*
>
> *Thank you, Lord. Amen.*

THE LOST ART
OF MENTORING

*For this reason I am sending to you Timothy, my son
whom I love, who is faithful in the Lord.*

1 CORINTHIANS 4:17

*M*entoring seems to be a lost art. The American Heritage
Dictionary describes a mentor as "a wise and trusted counselor
or teacher." The New Testament portrays Paul as a mentor to the
younger Timothy. Paul took Timothy under his wing and taught
him by word and example the ways of God. He took him on
mission trips and at times sent Timothy out alone as his repre-
sentative to the churches. Paul allowed his own life to speak to
Timothy of the calling that God places on those in leadership.

When I was growing up my pastor, Edwin Gunn, was a valued spiritual mentor. I could ask him about anything concern-
ing my relationship with Christ, and he would sit down, open
the Bible, and teach me what God had to say about life. He gave
me many opportunities to minister to others and was always
encouraging and supportive. As an emotional adolescent, if I got
a little off base with some of my ideas, he would very gently steer
me back to the Word of God.

When I was a student at London Bible College the school
principal, Gilbert Kirby, took up where Edwin left off. Though
he was a busy man, he always took time to help me work out my
faith. I'm sure many of my questions were naive and immature,
but he never for a moment made me feel childish. I remember
going to his office one day and telling him that I was leaving

school because the world was going to hell; what good was I doing here in a classroom learning about the Protestant Reformation? The subject matter was going to help no one, including me. He listened and we then talked about what God might be doing in me in these school years to make me a more effective servant when I graduated. I'm sure he sometimes smiled to himself when I left his study, but I never sensed a patronizing attitude.

I remember two great things about these men: (1) Though they were busy, juggling many demands of ministry, they took time to help me process my faith; (2) their lives spoke volumes to me about the way a man or woman of God should live.

In his book *The Charismatic Christ* Archbishop Ramsey says, "A terrible judgment rests upon the man of God who is unable to give help or guidance because he has ceased to be a man of prayer himself."

In the church today there is a tremendous need for mentoring. Alongside seminars or classes on successful church planting or effective preaching, maybe we need counsel on how to live and how to love.

There is no greater mentor than Christ. He lived for three years with twelve men. Every day, by what he said and what he did, he taught them what it looked like to serve God with all one's heart. Paul followed in his footsteps and loved Timothy and built him up in the faith.

And we also can follow their lead, coming alongside someone, possibly a younger person, to steady that person's walk in Christ. It may be inconvenient, frustrating, and time-consuming. But someday someone might thank you, as I thank my pastor and principal, who gave me time and wisdom.

A valued treasure.

Heart to heart, face to face,
we have found a treasure that nothing can replace.
Heart to heart, tried and true,
Love is born the day that love lays down for you.

Lord,
Thank you that you are our mentor. Teach us to lay our lives
down for one another. Amen.

THE FRIENDSHIP OF BOOKS

I devoted myself to study and to explore by wisdom all that is done under heaven.

ECCLESIASTES 1:13

*M*any of my best friends have more than two hundred pages! I have loved books since I was a child. I love to read and I still love to have books read to me. As Christmas approaches, Barry and I dig into our Christmas book box and read to one another. On alternating nights we take turns picking a story; we light a fire, sit back, and read or listen as we are carried away by *A Child's Christmas in Wales* by Dylan Thomas, *A Christmas Carol* by Charles Dickens, or the story of the Bethlehem birth.

Recently I was looking for a book to give to a friend. Glancing through shelf upon shelf of books I realized how many old friends I have. I noted *Hind's Feet on High Places* by Hannah Hurnard. When I was a student at London Bible College, that book helped chart me through some very difficult waters. I dusted off my collection of the works of Isaac Bashevis Singer and Thomas Hardy; both had enlarged my understanding of human nature. I picked up one of many volumes of poetry and read again the wonderful poem of Rudyard Kipling titled "If." I looked at the stiff binding of *War and Peace* and wondered why I've never been able to wade my way through it. My C. S. Lewis library is right on the front shelf; different books of his have touched me at various seasons of life. I love *The Lion, the Witch and the Wardrobe.* I love his poetry; I love *Surprised by Joy* and *The Screwtape Letters,* but my favorite of all is *Till We Have Faces,* a Greek myth retold.

So many books have influenced me. I love television and movies, but for me nothing will ever take the place of a good book. I have learned from the wisdom and folly of real and fictional characters. I have shed tears with weeping poets and laughed aloud at humorous or joyous scenarios. When I am sad or discouraged, I can pick up a book, find a quiet corner, and be reminded by the author of who I am in Christ. When I am being selfish or cold, a book can touch my heart and melt me to my knees.

I love to study the lives of men and women of faith who have gone before me. The light of their stories still shines, challenging me to live a life worthy of the calling of Christ. I pray that what I learn from the lives of others will be used by God to make me a more compassionate woman, more willing to serve, more grateful to God and of more use to others.

Sometime, when you feel a little lonely, consider a visit to your local bookstore. Ask a trusted friend to recommend a book that will lighten your spirit, deepen your wisdom, or widen your vision.

Find a new friend—in a book.

There are friends waiting on every shelf!

Lord,
Thank you that in a world without direction you have left us signs along the way through the lives of those who have gone before us or who walk beside us. Teach us to hear your voice through them. Thank you for good books that can be faithful friends and teachers.

Amen.

A PIECE OF HEAVEN

And when she finds it, she calls her friends and neighbors together and says, "Rejoice with me; I have found my lost coin."

LUKE 15:9

I was searching through my box of photographs to find a picture of our dog's first birthday party to send to my mom. (I had recently told her on the phone that Bentley wore a party hat and had a cake with candles; I wanted to back up this ridiculous assertion with physical evidence.)

Before I had unearthed Bentley's picture, I found three photographs that caught my attention. I made myself a cup of tea and sat outside in the shade to study them more closely. They captured three different occasions separated by some time. But many of the faces were the same.

The first one was a bridal shower that my friend Marlene threw for me. There were perhaps twenty women huddled together to get in the picture, laughing as we all tried to make sure our hair was unmussed and our skirts were straight. I thought back to that day and remembered that after all the laughter and silly games and cake, these friends gathered around me and prayed for Barry and me. After most of the women left, a few lingered to talk.

The second was a surprise birthday party I threw for Barry. I rented a karaoke machine, which was a huge mistake. Barry found one tape that was in his key and sang "Rhinestone Cowboy" over and over until we all wanted to put a bullet through the speakers! The photo showed friends watching Barry and laughing as he tried to give Glen Campbell a run for his money. I remembered that after most people had gone home, a few of us sat around the fire, drinking coffee and talking about our lives.

The third was taken at our home, not long ago. Barry decided to honor the fact that I was turning forty and pregnant. On my birthday when I came home from an afternoon out with a couple of my close friends, I found thirty-five people in the house—with gifts for me and for the little one.

I looked at these photographs and thought again of how rich I am. On each occasion after the larger crowd had left, a few of us lingered around the fire for several hours. I thought of the words of C. S. Lewis: "Is there any pleasure on earth as great as a circle of Christian friends by a fire?" Each of my close friends brings something different to me. Barry is always making me laugh; he is so honest and real. Marlene, keenly aware of global concerns, "takes us" around the world and reminds us of the church in other countries. Frank draws us back to Scripture and holds the Word up as a plumb line to our ideas. Cindy is a straight arrow whose passion for purity flies straight and true. Sara's commitment to integrity and compassion cuts through our wordy rhetoric. Dan's love of books spreads a feast before us. Marilyn's warm and generous heart welcomes us all, and Steve's quiet wisdom anchors us. We are richer together than we are apart. Because of what each person brings, our lives are deepened and our vision enlarged.

C. S. Lewis said that we picture lovers face to face but friends side by side; I think that is even more true when Christ is at the center of our lives—when we are all heading in the same direction with one heart and mind, to become more like Christ.

I can survive without a lot of things, but to live without friends would be to live in a cave and never see the sunrise again.

We need the input, the challenge, the encouragement, even the "spur" that comes from others in community. We call on each other to celebrate and we call on each other to weep. Surely this is a treasure above others, a piece of heaven, a promise of what is to come.

> *I see in you a piece of heaven never seen before.*
> *I laugh with you and celebrate the good things*
> *   at your door.*
> *I weep with you when sorrow lays its hand upon*
> *   your head.*
> *And I am rich beyond this life for those whom*
> *   I call friend.*
>
> *Amen.*

PART FIVE

SOLITUDE

You cannot escape from yourself; for God has singled you out.

DIETRICH BONHOEFFER,
LIFE TOGETHER

*T*he view from the top of the cliffs is breathtaking. On a clear day when the sun is beating down on the lush Cornwall soil and the gulls are dancing, there is no more beautiful place than England. I sat on the grass as bees gently hummed around me, landing on the purple clover. I made a mental note to buy some local honey. I closed my eyes and listened to the sound of the ocean as it broke against the rocks below.

It was an unusually quiet day at this tourist attraction, and I was grateful for the peace. I was at Land's End, the most southerly tip of England. A plaque on a house there reads "This is the last house in England and the first." I thought about that for a while. Of course, it all depends on which direction you are facing. If you stand with your back to Cornwall and your face to France, indeed it is the last house in England. But if you stand with your back to the ocean and your face toward England, it is just the beginning.

Several years later while driving to a radio interview in southern California, I tuned in to a religious broadcaster whose show was already in progress. "Some of you today, my friends, are at wit's end," he said. "You have done everything you know to do, and there is nowhere left to turn but to God."

As I listened, my thoughts went back to the plaque on that little house on the English coast. Again I thought, *It is all a matter of what direction you are facing.* There have been times when I have fallen exhausted at the feet of Christ with nowhere left to turn—but I have found it to be a beginning and not the end. I may have been at the end of my ideas and my self-confidence, the end of my ability, but in truth I was at a new beginning. The beginning of listening to God, being directed by him, finding rest in him.

This deep communion with God happens only when we are alone. I used to hate being alone and quiet. I would have the radio or the television on, the sound filling every room as I moved around my home. Not anymore. Solitude is a gift. It is a gift I received at a very high price, and one I do not take lightly. In the midst of the greatest crisis in my life, when I was at my wit's end, I shifted direction—from reliance on my own ability to total dependence on Christ. Suddenly I opened my eyes and the view had changed. I had turned my back on the jagged rocks below, and I was facing a lush, green carpet spreading out for miles before me. Solitude is good for the soul. It is there that we find peace and perspective for our lives. More important, it is there that we meet Christ in all his risen glory and are lifted from our fears and failures to the Everlasting Arms.

PRACTICE
MAKES PERFECT PEACE

The LORD is my shepherd, I shall not be in want. He makes me lie down in green pastures, he leads me beside quiet waters.

PSALM 23:1–2

*G*ood morning, Sheila. My name is Al."

"Good morning. I hope you had a good breakfast," I said making a halfhearted attempt at humor.

"I have a strong stomach."

This was my first driving lesson—at age twenty-seven! After my father died we didn't have a car. We rode the bus. As a newlywed Mom had tried to learn to drive, but because Dad— the teacher—was fiercely protective of his vehicles, I don't think she received much encouragement.

Driving looked so easy. I sat in the driver's seat and surveyed all the bells and whistles that one had to master to get a license; I listened as Al talked me through lesson one. Then came the big moment, turning the engine on. I felt like James Bond behind the wheel of an Aston Martin as I edged the car out of its parking space. We were on a quiet street in Costa Mesa, California, when Al made his first big mistake.

"You can go a little faster than this," he said.

"Hold onto your hat, Al!" I replied, as I lived out my Indy 500 dreams.

Halfway through the lesson Al asked if we could stop for coffee. I thought this was his normal practice. But as he sat in the coffee shop fanning himself with the menu, I wondered if I was a bit too much for Al.

It amazed me—how difficult it was to get it all right. It looked easy, but trying to get my hands to do what my brain was telling them at the right time—this was very hard.

"Will you be my instructor all the time?" I asked as we headed back to the car.

"Afraid so. I mean, yes," he said.

I remember thinking that I would never get it right; it would never come naturally to me, but I was wrong. All it took was consistent practice and commitment—and a few unscheduled coffee stops for Al.

A similar discipline is required in solitude. It is a learned discipline. Our environment offers any number of noisy options to keep us constantly entertained. We have forgotten how to be quiet. When I first began to give myself to the discipline of solitude I despaired of ever being able to quiet my mind. I would turn the radio or TV off and sit for a while. My mind would wander all over the place. I found myself thinking about what I could make for dinner, and did Lou Anne's carrot soup recipe call for one or two leeks? I was repeatedly discouraged, wanting to quit, reasoning that this was simply not the way for me to fellowship with God. But I didn't give up. I kept trying. After a while I began to relax into being alone with God. I left all my lists and requests behind. This was time for quiet, not for petition.

My times of silence before God are very important to me now. I put everything else down, every word away, and I am with the Lord. When I'm quiet, life falls into perspective for me. I have a very active mind and I'm a worrier, but in those moments when I choose to put that away, I rest beside the Shepherd in still places.

Why don't you give yourself a gift today? Turn off the television or the car stereo, put down the newspaper or the business plan, and in the quietness, rest for a while beside the Shepherd of your soul.

The only sound that visits me is the rapid whir of wings,
a hummingbird caught in the air. I turn from
*   other things*
to rest in you; you quieten me. I lay my burdens down,
and by the river's edge I sit dressed in a silent gown.

Amen.

SMALL HARBORS

He who dwells in the shelter of the Most High will rest in the shadow of the Almighty.

PSALM 91:1

Generally these days, when I go on a retreat, I travel some distance and am one of the guest speakers. In my teens and twenties I often gathered with a small group, enjoying the intensity of a few days together on retreat, most often out of town. Now I find "small harbors" as often as I can. By this I mean that instead of setting off on big trips, I have a lot of little departures. I find them in my day. I'm driving to the airport, and my car becomes a little harbor for quiet fellowship with God. I'm walking the dog, and as he sets off across the hillside I find a "small harbor" and sit down for a while. There is something very settling about a harbor, it steadies the boat.

A few years ago I was asked to go to Belfast, Northern Ireland, to perform a concert with my band. We sailed from Stranraer on the west coast of Scotland to Larne on the Irish coast. Despite the horror that Belfast has seen with bombings and riots, it is a beautiful city and its people have great hearts.

After the concert, as we sat in Larne harbor waiting for the boat to leave, we were all talking about the successful event and how much we enjoyed the people. It had taken me a long time to convince my saxophone player that he would be safe on this trip, but now that it was over and we were leaving, it was obvious to us all that we were carrying away a great memory.

Suddenly an announcement informed us that a storm had blown up; our boat would be the last one out that day. The captain gave a few other instructions about safety measures and then we set sail. Sitting in the harbor it was hard to believe that there was much trouble brewing, but once we were in the open sea, it was a different matter altogether. The boat began to tip from side to side. Dishes from the dining room were flying all over the place. Two of the band members were hanging over the side—rather the worse for wear. The crossing lasted only about an hour but there were many green faces as we docked in Stranraer. Once in that harbor it was quiet again, and the roller-coaster sea trip seemed unreal.

Harbors are like that. They give you a little shelter, a break in the maelstrom of the rough waters.

We don't always have time for grand departures to wonderful retreats or resorts where we can be refreshed and renewed. That is why I treasure small harbors. They are all around us waiting to let us catch our breath before the next wind carries us away.

Resting in you, Lord Jesus,
safe from the storms at sea,
tucked in your arms and sheltered,
here you will steady me.

Amen.

STILL ENOUGH TO HEAR

On my bed I remember you; I think of you through the watches of the night.

PSALM 63:6

*O*ne of my greatest vices is that I talk before I think. (I remember the words of a godly counselor who told me the world would be a better place if I could cut in half what I had to say.) I have opinions on everything and love to give them regular airings. I process information very quickly and am ready to respond almost immediately, but I am slowly learning the benefit of taking time to meditate, to really listen, and to be changed by what I hear.

I think we in the church community have become shy of meditation because of our horror of all things that sound like the new age movement. But meditation is a spiritual discipline, a gift to the church, that we as the people of God have been called to. In the book *The Way to Freedom*, I've read that when Dietrich Bonhoeffer was asked why he meditated he responded simply, "Because I am a Christian."

Consider the words of Psalm 48:9: "Within your temple, O God, we meditate on your unfailing love."

In *The Imitation of Christ*, Thomas à Kempis describes meditation as "a familiar friendship with Jesus." I like that. He talks about the end results of meditation—being able to hear God's voice and obey his word. "A familiar friendship" evolves as we spend time with someone—not just talking but watching and listening, observing how that person reacts, learning what he or she likes and doesn't like. A familiar and strong bond builds between two people. You know your friend very well.

A simple example comes to mind. Recently Barry and I were flying back to Los Angeles after an exhausting trip. Our flight had been delayed for four hours in Chicago. By the time we finally took off on the last leg home, we were bone tired and we hadn't eaten in hours. Then we were stuck right at the back of the plane—where people lean on you as they wait to use the rest room! By the time the flight attendant got to us with the meals, she was out of what Barry wanted. Frustrated, he gave up and said he didn't want anything to eat, thank you.

I thought about this for a moment and then asked if we could please have his meal. When that tray was put down in front of him, he smiled at me and said, "You know me so well"—meaning I knew he was really hungry but just too tired to shift in his mind and accept a meal that wasn't his first choice; I knew he needed to—wanted to—eat.

I know Barry so well because I've spent so much time with him. And I get to know God as I spend time with him, meditating on his Word. Meditating on the Word of God is a very different discipline than reading the Bible or praying. When I meditate, I take perhaps just one verse and sit with it for a while and ask God to speak to me. I might keep it in my mind for the whole day.

Consider the verse "Perfect love casts out fear" (1 John 4:18 NKJV). It immediately speaks to me. But as I sit with it for a long time, so much more comes to my heart. I ask, "What is perfect love?" I think about my own fears and what it is like to let God's love touch them and take them away. As I sit with God I experience a new level of intimacy and worship, a deeper confidence and trust in him.

Mary, the mother of Jesus, accepted the angel's message to her and pondered his words in her heart. That is meditation— to reflect or consider with thoroughness and care. God's Word is life to us and yet we spend so little time truly taking it in.

As we meditate on God's Word, we become familiar with God's heart and his ways; as we do so, we will change. The purpose of meditation is not simply to make us feel good in a noisy world; it is not a self-absorbed agenda. Rather, as we shut our mind in with God and reflect on his words, we will know him and be changed by him—and that is the purpose of our lives.

"Be still, and know that I am God."

Lord, grant me the stillness of heart and mind that I will know you in ways deeper than I have ever known you before. Amen.

BE STILL

Be still, and know that I am God.

PSALM 46:10

*I*n my second trimester of pregnancy I experienced severe shortness of breath. My doctor referred me to a pulmonary specialist, who arranged for tests. "I've scheduled you for noninvasive venous studies—this afternoon," he said. "They will detect any blood clots in your legs. If we find anything, I'll have you admitted right away."

As I lay on the hospital bed waiting for the technician to begin the tests, my mind started racing:

"Did I leave enough food out for the dog?"

"I should have picked up Barry's shirts from the dry cleaners yesterday."

"I'm starving."

"I have a speaking engagement this weekend. I can't be in the hospital."

I looked at the machines around me and wondered what this day had in store. Then I listened to the sounds coming from the room next door. Sitting in the waiting room, I'd seen the patient going in. She seemed to be in severe pain. Her husband helped her with every labored step.

Now, from next door, I could hear an ultrasound machine. As it scanned, it amplified the sound of blood pouring through veins and arteries. The sound—like the ocean on an angry day—was unnerving as it washed into the quiet of my room. I closed my eyes. When I opened them again they rested on a poster on the wall in front of me. It said, "We carry within us the wonders we seek without us."

I was struck by the simple beauty and truth of those words. How often had I looked outside of myself for peace and joy and intimacy in my relationship with Christ, as if it were a gift that someone else might give me? We think that if we just read the right book or attend the right conference or travel to the church where everyone says that God is showing up in unprecedented ways, then we will find that wonder—that joy—we are seeking. But I have discovered that this is not true. That joy and peace that we go off hunting for are always experienced secondhand. We have a divine gift through the sacrifice of Christ; this means we can come directly into the presence of God by ourselves. True joy does not lie outside of us. It is not at the end of a telephone line or a new job offer or a new partner; it lies in the stillness of our moments with Christ.

I thought about the woman in the next room. Her blood is always pumping in her veins, but she can't hear it; it is a hidden world. Only when she lies in a quiet room with the world tuned out and a special machine turned on does the unheard world that is always there become the most present thing. So it is with Christ. That is the gift of solitude. When we get away from the invasive noise and activity of this world that makes so many demands on our time and attention, when we tune into our relationship with Christ, we discover the wonder that we are waiting for. We can wait for wonder to come knocking at our door. But if we will be quiet and listen, we will hear it knocking at our hearts.

> Dear Lord,
> In the stillness I wait for you;
> in the stillness you wait for me,
> for there I will know in my soul,
> in the depths of my heart,
> that you alone are God. Amen.

STANDING ALONE TOGETHER

Now you are the body of Christ, and each one of you is a part of it.

1 CORINTHIANS 12:27

In Letters and Papers from Prison, the German theologian Dietrich Bonhoeffer wrote, "Let him who cannot be alone beware of community."

I have thought about this interesting statement for some time. At first it seemed contradictory. Surely it is the lonely who need to be in community. But I now see Bonhoeffer's point. Those who cannot be alone with themselves expect others to be their lives, and no one can do that for another human being.

There are so many weak, malnourished believers who have never grown in Christ. What happens when they are in community? You have a room full of needy children who are expecting someone else to help them make it through this life, who have no skills to enable them to resolve conflict and nothing to give to others. I believe that is what Bonhoeffer warns about.

We are all called to stand up and be who we are in Christ. That is something that we find out on our own with the Lord. God will use others to help us, but each one of us came into this world alone and we will all stand alone before God when we die.

Standing alone is vital for our spiritual health. We are urged to pray for one another but that does not mean that we abdicate our individual commitment to pray for ourselves. When we, by ourselves, know who we are in Christ, when we have a strong personal relationship with him, then we have so much to offer each other.

Sometimes we want to step in and rescue a fellow believer from any discomfort that may come in the maturing process. But I'm reminded of an insight I've learned from nature. Baby birds can die when someone steps up and cracks open the eggs at hatching time. The birds need the pecking and effort, which gives them fortitude. The struggle builds into them what they will need to survive in the world; outside interference—though well intentioned—can write a death certificate for the birds.

I used to think that I could carry a few of my more wounded sisters over the finishing line, but I realize now what a disservice that is. It is not love. We are not called to take each other's burdens away; we are called to share that burden, to walk alongside. We are called to encourage one another to keep our eyes on Jesus, the author and finisher of our faith.

As we stand alone with Christ and receive from him, we are able to be part of a living, growing community of faith. Drawing our strength from him in solitude, we can know who we are and what he has called us to, and we can bring that with us each time we are together—as fellow members of the body of Christ. How rich a life—as individuals and as a community—that would be.

From that first cry as we are broken into the world
we are alone.
At that last sigh as we make our journey home
we are alone.

Teach us, Lord, to stand alone so that we can stand
together. Amen.

PART SIX

DISCIPLINES

Why, then, are you afraid to take up your cross, which leads to the Kingdom? In the cross is salvation; in the cross is life, in the cross is strength of mind; in the cross is joy of spirit.

THOMAS À KEMPIS

I met my friend Moira in the school parking lot, and there we waited for two other students and our teacher Mr. McDougal. It was Friday, and we were setting off on a camping/survival trip as part of the Duke of Edinburgh's Award program. Every year the queen's husband presented gold medals to students who had undertaken various assignments, from community service to survival trips, such as the one we were about to embark on. Once we were all in the school van, Mr. McDougal addressed us.

"Did you bring everything on your list?" he asked. Each of us had been assigned to bring specific items we would need as a team.

"Yes, Mr. McDougal," we all chanted.

Deep in the Scottish countryside, he left us by the side of the road and told us that he would see us on Sunday evening.

We set off in high spirits. It was a beautiful day, and I love to walk across the fields, over the hills, and feel the soft grass or springy gorse beneath my feet. After a few hours, however, the sky began to cloud over, and it started to rain. Very quickly, it was pouring.

"Okay, Moira," Sandra said, "bring out the waterproofs."

With rain running into our shoes, we all waited for Moira to produce the expected rolled-up jackets.

"Hurry up, Moira!" I yelled. "It's getting worse."

"I don't have them," she wailed back.

"What do you mean you don't have them? They were on your list!" Linda said indignantly.

"But it didn't look like rain," Moira replied.

We ran for shelter in an old barn in the corner of a field and waited for the rain to stop. We were now soaking wet and miserable. By the time the rain stopped, we had lost two hours.

"We're still three hours away from the youth hostel," Linda said. "We'd better make a fire and cook our dinner outside instead of waiting till we get there. Sheila, pass me the matches."

"I don't have them," I answered quietly, trying to make it sound like no big deal.

"You were supposed to bring them!"

"I know," I replied, "but I thought that if we were at the youth hostel for our meal, we wouldn't need them."

"So what do we do now?" Sandra asked. "Starve to death?"

We ate cold beans out of a can and set off toward the youth hostel.

"We'll have our dessert when we get there," Moira said. "You did bring dessert?" she asked Linda.

"Yes I did," Linda replied with a touch of pride.

Finally we saw the lights of the hostel, and we checked in for the night.

"See you in the kitchen in ten minutes," Moira and I shouted, as Sandra and Linda headed off to create our dessert.

We could hear them shouting at one another from down the corridor.

"What's wrong?" I asked, as I stuck my head in the door.

"She didn't bring the whisk!" Sandra pointed an accusing finger at Linda.

"Well, you didn't bring the bowl!" Linda shot back.

By the time Mr. McDougal collected us on Sunday night we all had our tails between our legs. We had not been prepared for our trip.

Imagine our lives like that. We do not know how long the trip will take or how much ground we will cover in any given day. We plan an itinerary; we are guided by experience, but unforeseen challenges, problems, and questions arise regularly. What can we know for sure about this journey? How can we prepare ourselves to face whatever lies ahead? What do we do when we face a divide in the road and both paths look good? Or how do we find strength to take the more difficult path when we know it is the right way—but we are so weary? What do we do when it becomes apparent that we are lost or on the wrong road? How do we live now in a way that will help us in the next leg of our journey? What are the daily disciplines that we can choose, so that when the sky gets cloudy for a while we can walk by faith and not by sight?

In my own life I am discovering how important daily spiritual discipline is in terms of the little choices I continually make. As we make small, apparently unimportant, unnoticed, right choices, we align ourselves with who we are—the body of Christ.

We don't talk much about spiritual disciplines—but we should. God has promised to provide help for us on our journey but we cannot expect to stand with weak, untrained knees. We wouldn't think of sending an eighteen-year-old soldier into a bloody battle with shorts, a T-shirt, and a backpack filled with candy bars. But is this what we do in terms of our own souls? Most of us are lazy when it comes to our souls. Feeling confident that we will get into heaven, we allow the world's amusements and noise and obligations to press upon us and distract us from what really counts.

The rusted gate to the spiritual disciplines may look uninviting, but if you press on through you will discover a world that will equip you for your journey in a way that you never dreamed.

FOR GOD ALONE

Therefore, I urge you, brothers, in view of God's mercy, to offer your bodies as living sacrifices, holy and pleasing to God—this is your spiritual act of worship.

ROMANS 12:1

*I*n the New Testament we are called to be *living* sacrifices. That's in contrast to the *dead* sacrifices of the Old Testament, where a young animal would be killed. After its blood was drained, it would be offered up to God as a sacrifice. A slain animal no longer has a choice, but you and I do. Think about it: A living sacrifice can crawl back off the altar if it gets too hot. It requires a daily choice to stay on that altar no matter how intense the heat.

Paul says that, in view of God's mercy, we should offer our lives to him in a way that costs us. True love involves sacrifice. That is where discipline comes in. Sometimes I don't feel like praying or opening my Bible. And at times I have reasoned that because I am free in Christ, under grace not law, it is okay for me to slack off and not push it.

But then I think of my relationship with my husband. I am sure there are days when he comes home, feeling too tired—after a long workday and a long drive—to talk to me or be loving or kind. But he chooses to. Some days after sitting at my computer all day, I'll look at the clock and realize that I'd better get a move on to fix dinner and fix myself before Barry comes home. I could think, "Oh well, he's my husband; he'll understand that I'm too busy to take care of that." But that would be foolish and selfish behavior. Because he loves me, he gives himself to me even when he is tired; I know at times it's a sacrifice. Because I love him, I give myself to him; and yes, sometimes it's a sacrifice. (It's easier to look like Phyllis Diller on an off day.) Why would we offer anything less to the Lord?

It's easy to forget that we are called to bless God with our lives. We think that God is there to bless us; we think there should be some benefit to us at every moment. God does not exist just to make our lives better; we exist so that we can learn to love and worship him in spirit and in truth. Love that involves no sacrifice at all is not love; it is cannibalism, feasting on someone else for what we can get out of it.

Discipline has been a hard lesson for me to learn. It doesn't come naturally to me, but I have come to appreciate its gifts. I love to write. Some days when I sit down at my desk, the words flow so easily and it's pure joy. Some days I don't feel inspired at all, but I've learned the value of giving myself to my work anyway. At the end of a hard day, when I feel I have had to push myself through, I feel a tremendous satisfaction, knowing that I didn't waste the day. Similarly, when I give myself to worship when I would rather turn on the television or read a book, I often rejoice, realizing that these moments are some of the most special times I have with the Lord. As I pull my mind and heart away from myself and tune in to the greatness and goodness of God, my faith is matured. I delight in what is right and honorable. God is more than worthy of the disciplined offering of our lives. He never holds himself back from us, and when we give ourselves to him, we present worship with flesh on it, a gift with content, words undergirded by our lives.

"Therefore, I urge you, brothers, in view of God's mercy, to offer your bodies as living sacrifices, holy and pleasing to God—this is your spiritual act of worship."

Come before him now
offering your soul in worship
giving back the life he gives us
honoring the one who loves us.
Come before him now in worship
Holy is the Lord.

Amen.

PRAYER
CHANGES THINGS

If you remain in me and my words remain in you,
ask whatever you wish, and it will be given you.

JOHN 15:7

"Prayer changes things." That was the badge I wore on my jacket as a sixteen-year-old. I then viewed prayer as some type of external influence; we could align our hearts with God's heart and pray toward a change in a circumstance or person. But over the last few years I have discovered that what is most changed by prayer is the one who is praying. I see that prayer changes me. I can't stay the same when I pray. If I feel anger or resentment toward someone, I can't pray for that person and still hold on to the intensity of my emotion. Presenting a person or situation to God changes how I view it. I start with one stance, but as I spend time with God looking at the situation, I find that the world shifts a little. I'm given new perspective on what I see.

For two years I have had a hard time forgiving a friend who walked away from me when I really needed him. I couldn't understand why he was so distant and cold. I found it hard to pray for him; every time I tried to pray my feelings got in the way; I wanted him to know how much he had hurt me. I wanted him to hurt as he had hurt me. Yet I knew this was wrong, and my unforgiving spirit was affecting my life. And I kept thinking of the verse, "Anyone who claims to be in the light but hates his brother is still in the darkness" (1 John 2:9).

I felt stuck. My friend had no desire to be reconciled to me or to talk to me about the distance between us. I couldn't seem to throw off this "stone" that was dragging me down. So I began to seriously pray for him. I forgave him, not because I felt any forgiveness, but because Christ has forgiven me. I prayed that God would bless him and bring him closer to Christ every day. I prayed this for months. At times I would think I was making real progress, and then his name would be mentioned, maybe someone telling me that he had said something negative about me, and all the old feelings would come rushing back. But I would stop, grab hold of my heart, and pray for him again.

Over time I realized that God was changing my heart. I began to see this person as more than just the cause of hurt. I could remember his gifts and good qualities. He became a whole person in my mind again rather than just the perpetrator of one act. I still don't know if and when I will be reconciled with my friend, but I know that I am not the same person who began to pray for him two years ago.

Without the call to discipline I would have given up a long time ago. I would have seen our estrangement as his problem and attempted to move on in my life. But how can I remain in Christ and hate my brother? How can I expect God to hear and answer my prayers if I hold onto such a cold place in my heart? When I started to pray for him, my motive was that God would change him. That was my whole intent. As I continued in prayer with discipline as a dear and trusted friend, I saw that it is God's heart to change me.

If you feel stuck bring your whole self to Christ, not just the problem, but you. Ask God to change your heart. Commit yourself to pray to that end. It's God's heart to give good gifts to his children.

Prayer, a gently crafted tool
chisels at my heart
working on the stony ground,
shaping me till love is found
where fear and anger lay.

Thank you, Lord, for the gift of prayer. Amen.

RENEW YOUR MIND

Do not conform any longer to the pattern of this world, but be transformed by the renewing of your mind. Then you will be able to test and approve what God's will is—his good, pleasing and perfect will.

ROMANS 12:2

*F*ifty percent of your grade will be based on your research paper, which must be turned in two weeks before the end of the semester."

I sat in seminary class in church history and listened to Professor Nathan Feldmeth as I scanned the list of possible research topics. The paper had to be twenty-five pages long and include a bibliography of reference material.

For the next few nights I sat at my desk at home and wrestled with the task of writing this paper. Then, after the next class, I asked the professor if I could talk to him. "I don't know how to do this," I admitted.

"What do you mean?" he asked kindly.

"Well, I've never written a paper for a graduate class, and I honestly don't know where to start."

For thirty minutes Nate sat with me and went over each step: how to research, how to catalog the research, how the finished paper should look. He helped me to understand how to access knowledge, how to read a book so that I will understand it, grasp hold of what is being said, and then determine if I agree with the writer. I left that meeting grateful for his guidance and guidelines. I felt less ignorant, more confident that I could take one step at a time.

In all of life, study is a faithful friend if we learn its ways. I see that a great deal of damage is done not by evil but by ignorance. Christ tells us that we will know the truth and the truth will set us free (John 8:32), but so often we don't know what the truth is. We don't know how to dig it out. In Romans Paul tells us that our lives are to be transformed by the renewing of our minds. But if we have no firm grasp on what God's Word says, how can we be changed by it?

I think we Christians have become lazy. We would rather read a book about how someone else became closer to God than spend time alone with him ourselves. We would rather listen to someone else's interpretation of the Word of God than read it for ourselves. And yet we alone are accountable for what we believe. We can't stand before God on the day of judgment and explain that our incredible ignorance is our pastor's fault. It is our responsibility to access God's Word for ourselves.

Think about how much damage is done by ignorance. So many marriages break up because the couple didn't have a clue how to communicate. Now, as I enter the final trimester of my pregnancy, I am keenly aware of parental responsibility. Though we are dismayed by many differing opinions on the right way to raise a child, Barry and I are reading all the how-to books we can—and then we will rely on God to guide us to make good choices.

Yes, study is a faithful friend if we will learn its disciplined ways.

As a Christian I am passionately committed to study. I want to know for myself what God says. I want to know the things that make him happy and the things that break his heart. I want to know how to live a life that will please him. How can I do that if I don't study his words to me?

There is nothing in life more important than understanding God's truth and being changed by it, so why are we so casual about accepting the popular theology of the moment without checking it out for ourselves? God has given us a mind so that we can learn and grow. As his people we have a great responsibility and wonderful privilege of growing in our understanding of him. If marriages could be saved and children's lives made richer by study and understanding and change, think of the impact on the church if we as individual Christians befriended the spiritual discipline of study.

I like to take a passage of Scripture or a good Christian book and write down what strikes me or what questions I have as I read. When I get together with my friends, I'll throw these thoughts into the arena and we'll wrestle with them to grasp hold of what God is saying to us. When we dig deep, there are hidden treasures to be found.

> *Your Word is like a flaming sword*
> *A sharp and mighty arrow*
> *A wedge that cleaves the rock;*
> *That word can pierce through heart and marrow*
> *Oh, send it forth o'er all the earth*
> *To purge unrighteous leaven*
> *And cleanse our hearts for heaven.*
>
> CARL GARVE

THE TRUTH
WILL SET YOU FREE

Buy the truth and do not sell it; get wisdom, discipline and understanding.

PROVERBS 23:23

I want you to take this blank journal and keep an honest and fearless inventory of your life, Sheila."

I was working with a Christian counselor and had expressed to her that I was at times frustrated by my lack of progress in certain areas. "When I get tired or overworked," I said, "I fall back into the same old patterns of withdrawing into myself and feeling resentful."

"I think it would help you to write down what you think and what you feel. Seeing it on paper will help you to bring it all before Christ and ask for his help."

At first I found this hard to do. What would someone think if someone got hold of it? I felt tempted to tidy up my thoughts even for God—until I realized how pointless that would be.

But now I see that this risky discipline has had a marked impact on my life. Taking a cold hard look at what is true about myself mirrored back on paper holds me accountable to what is true. When I see it there, it's pointless to say that it's not a problem. I sincerely want to be more like Christ; that is my goal. Hiding from what is true about myself will never help me in that journey.

Facing the truth about myself involves accepting responsibility for myself and my actions. I must stop unhealthy patterns of blaming other people for the inconsistencies in my own life.

When I react a certain way because of people around me, I am choosing to be a victim to the whims and behavior of others. As a Christian I am called to be above that.

It takes courage and honesty to grab hold of the things in our lives that are dishonoring to God and give God permission to shine his light on them—but that is how we are called to live.

Looking at things in the light has a way of reducing many of them to an appropriate size. I lived most of my life plagued by vague fears and insecurities. When I try to identify and write them down I can look at them in the presence of God, and he brings his peace to my secret fears. They assume proper proportions. Unspoken fears can take on terrifying dimensions, but when brought into the open with God, his perfect love casts out our fear.

The Word of God exhorts us to get hold of wisdom and understanding, to know the truth, for he who knows the truth will be set free.

Stepping out of the shadows,
I bring my heart to you,
setting foot in the sunlight
with all the things that are true.
Trusting you in your wisdom
to mold me, to make me new.
Facing myself in the light of your grace,
bringing my life to you.
In Jesus' name,

Amen.

FOOT WASHING

After that, he poured water into a basin and began to wash his disciples' feet, drying them with the towel that was wrapped around him.

JOHN 13:5

*I*n one great selfless act, as he got down on his knees and washed the feet of his friends, Christ destroyed the concept of what's "appropriate." If one followed the rules of position and authority, he—the leader, the respected teacher and miracle worker—was the last person in the room who should have performed that menial task. In the final few hours with his twelve disciples—men who had been with him since the beginning of his ministry—he delivered a powerful punch to what true greatness really is.

We feel good about ourselves when others rush to serve us; we are relieved when someone else volunteers to do a job with no luster. Of all the patterns that Christ modeled for us, this seems to be our least favorite.

I've worked with many people over the last twenty years, and none has impressed me more in terms of simple humility than Cliff Richard. Cliff is a huge star, a household name in the rest of the world, although he is not as well known here in the U.S. During his career he has sold more singles than The Beatles, The Rolling Stones, and The Who combined, and he is a very committed Christian.

I first met him, and was awed by his talent, on a charity tour for a British relief agency, Tear Fund. I was with the band that opened for him. Then his gospel manager, Bill Latham, became my manager and Cliff and I became friends. When Cliff coproduced an album for me, I was amazed at his attitude. He was there on time every morning and stayed until every session was over. He sang all the backup vocals to save me money and because he thought that it would be fun. For a while I was his regular opening act, and he always made sure that I had everything I needed. All this goes to say that there was nothing of the "star" about him in how he lived. He was a brother in Christ.

A few years later I invited him to the Christian Artists' seminar in Colorado. One morning as we were out walking, a girl came up and asked for my autograph. As I signed her book I introduced Cliff. She said, "Oh, great to meet you. You're Sheila's backup vocalist!" He just smiled and said, "That's right." At peace with who he was, he felt no need to remind anyone of his renowned role.

To my view, Cliff's humility stands in stark contrast to what I see in the church in America. We are very impressed with "gifting." And the art of giving, of serving, of servanthood is way down the list of valued qualities. We live in a culture that encourages us to alienate ourselves from people perceived to be "beneath" us. Or at best we patronize them, allowing them to serve us. But Christ says, "I have set you an example that you should do as I have done for you. I tell you the truth, no servant is greater than his master, nor is a messenger greater than the one who sent him. Now that you know these things, you will be blessed if you do them" (John 13:15–17).

To gain perspective, I suggest we turn back to the spiritual disciplines. As we pray and meditate and study and simplify our lives, we get a sharper picture of what is true and what is of worth and what is self-indulgent garbage. Spending disciplined time alone with God gives us a picture of our own worthlessness and the awesome majesty of who we serve.

Lord, give me the heart of a servant, to love without limit, to give expecting nothing in return, to wash the tired feet and tired hearts of those around me as you have washed my soul. Amen.

PART SEVEN

HEALING

Be the goal of my pilgrimage and my rest by the way. Let my soul take refuge from the crowding turmoil of worldly thoughts beneath the shadow of your wings: let my heart, this sea of restless waves, find peace in you, O God. Amen.

St. Augustine

*T*he final box was sealed and the truck was loaded.

"See you in California!" the truck driver shouted as he pulled out of the driveway. We had been living in Nashville for a few months, and now we were getting in the car, heading back to the west coast. I looked at my husband and I looked at my cat and wondered which one of them would get tired of the drive first. Abigail, the cat, had a carrier in the backseat with a little blanket and some toys. We had a litter box on the floor that we figured she could use at stops.

Everything was fine for about forty miles, until Barry said that he could not stand Abigail's constant mewing. I thought, *This is going to be quite some trip. Forty miles down, only nineteen hundred and sixty to go.* We soon let Abby out of her cage, and she seemed to do better. Eventually she settled on the back window shelf and peace was restored—temporarily.

We drove for hours, until we were all exhausted and decided to look for a motel. Barry went in to register and get our room key. He returned to the car and said, "We have to pass the front desk and I'm not sure what their policy is on pets, so you'd better put Abigail inside your sweater."

He grabbed the bags and I duly stuffed Abby up my sweater. Everything was fine until we were halfway across the lobby and Barry frantically signaled that something was wrong.

I looked down and Abigail's big fluffy tail was sticking out of the bottom of my sweater. I tried to push it under, but then her head popped out of the top. By this point she was very cross, and I was laughing so hard I could hardly walk.

That was just day one.

By the end of the trip Abigail was lying on her back in the litter box, having abandoned all hope. Our cross-country trip might have been easier for Abigail if she had understood where we were going: to a new home that she would enjoy as much as her old one.

How often I have identified with my cat. There are times when I am tired of this journey, when I am simply worn out. As I have thought about what it means to heal a divided soul I realized that I struggle with not knowing where I am going. Oh, unlike Abigail, I know my ultimate destination; I know that when my life is over on this earth I will be with Christ forever. But until then . . . where is God leading me? Where will I be five years from now?

The disciples had similar questions. Thomas asked Jesus, "Lord, we don't know where you are going, so how can we know the way?"

Jesus answered, "I am the way and the truth and the life. No one comes to the Father except through me" (John 14:5–6).

I hear frustration in Thomas's voice. *You're not being fair here, Jesus. You want us to follow you, but you won't tell us where you are going. How can we do that? You're asking too much. Just tell us, Where are you going?*

Christ answered Thomas and he answers us: "You ask for the way, I AM THE WAY."

It would be so much easier if we were given a road map. It would make so much of the journey more bearable if we could see that the path that is painful for a time is leading somewhere and that it will get better. We don't have that. No believer who has gone before us has had that. There is no map; Christ is the Way.

Sometimes we feel so torn in two. Our human flesh cries out for comfort and direction, for some control, and yet we are called to live above that. That is why our lives are a journey of faith and why living is so hard sometimes. It's why our souls feel divided between the world and the way of the cross. Saint Augustine's prayer is so poignant. Surely, it is on the path with Christ that we will find rest. And when we are there, we will no longer wonder about God's will for our lives—we are living it.

To Will One Thing

Therefore, as God's chosen people, holy and dearly loved, clothe yourselves with compassion, kindness, humility, gentleness and patience.

COLOSSIANS 3:12

I looked at the clock in my car and realized that I had ten minutes to make a fifteen-minute trip—and I was out of gas. I pulled into a station. As I got out of the car, a young attendant approached. "Good morning, ma'am. Would you like me to check your oil today?"

"No thanks, I'm kind of in a hurry." The sign said "Pay before you pump." I thought I could save a few seconds, so I handed him a bill. "I want twenty dollars' worth. Would you take it in for me?"

"Sure would. It's going to be a hot one!" he said with a smile as he sauntered off at a snail's pace.

Oh man, I would have been quicker doing this myself, I thought. I watched as he stopped at another car to give someone directions, and by this time I was getting very frustrated. As the car pulled out, the guy turned and waved at me! I pointed to my watch.

"Yes, ma'am," he shouted.

Finally, when he'd paid the cashier, I lifted the pump to begin filling my car. He yelled at me to stop. "Hold up there," he said. "I'll be right over."

I ignored him and kept pumping my own gas. When he got to my car he reached over me and tried to take the pump from my hand.

"I've got it, thanks," I said.

"No ma'am, that's my job. I'm here to serve," he said with a big puppy grin.

By this point I was really cross as he was trying to wrestle the pump out of my clenched fist.

"I've got it!" I said and pulled harder on my end.

"It's my job!" he cried and pulled back.

"This is a self-serve aisle!" I yelled.

"I know it is, but I'm helping!" he pleaded pitifully.

"You're not helping, you're making me crazy!" I told him.

At that point he wandered away muttering to himself, and I drove away very late and very frustrated.

That evening I couldn't get this young man's face out of my mind. I ran the whole scenario over and over in my head trying to justify my lack of patience: I was late and he was so insistent. "It's fine to offer to help, but you can't push yourself on people," I reasoned.

Then I thought of Paul's words: "Clothe yourselves with compassion, kindness, humility, gentleness and patience" (Colossians 3:12).

I was so ashamed of myself. It is my expressed desire to live a life that demonstrates the love and compassion of Christ, but to that young man all I had exhibited was impatience and intolerance.

The next morning I drove past the gas station to see if he was there. I saw him on his hands and knees, polishing the bottom half of one of the pumps. I parked my car and walked over to him. "Do you remember me?" I asked.

He stopped what he was doing and looked up. "Sure I do," he said. "You're the lady who likes to pump her own gas."

"I'm here to ask you to forgive me for being so rude yesterday," I began. "You were trying to help me, and I was too stubborn to let you. I'm really sorry."

"That's okay," he said, as he stuck out his hand. "My name is James; I just like to do a good job."

I am still amazed at my lack of grace and kindness in the most simple of situations. I can go from speaking to a crowd about the love of God, feeling so close to heaven that it seems as if I have gold dust on my shoes to . . . driving in traffic and having someone cut me off—and I become a maniac.

All I know to do is (1) to keep bringing this rip in my soul to the foot of the cross and (2) whenever my unkindness touches the life of another to go to that person and ask forgiveness. It is my calling to treat every human being with grace and dignity, to treat every person, whether encountered in a palace or a gas station, as a life made in the image of God.

Breathe on me, breath of God,
Until my heart is pure,
Until with you I will one will,
To do and to endure.

EDWIN HATCH

TORN APART

But you, O Sovereign LORD, deal well with me for your name's sake; out of the goodness of your love, deliver me. For I am poor and needy, and my heart is wounded within me.

PSALM 109:21–22

I was waiting to board a flight from Dallas to Pittsburgh when I became aware of a little boy sitting beside a man I took to be his father. The boy had the airline's "unaccompanied minor" packet around his neck, so I knew he was flying alone. When it was time for children to board, the boy stood up and put his Barney backpack on. His dad walked with him to the door and bent down to hug him good-bye. When I got on the plane I realized that the child was sitting just across the aisle from me. He had his head down and his seatbelt tightly fastened. Later when we were served drinks, I noticed that he couldn't get his bag of nuts open, so I asked him if I could help. He handed me the packet. "That was my dad," he said. "I see him every summer."

"Did you have a good time?" I asked.

"Yes," he replied. Then he turned his face away, toward the window, and said, "I'm not crying."

My heart ached for that little boy. He was only about six years old and already his life was torn in two and his heart was broken. I wondered if he carried the burden of blaming himself for his parents' separation, as so many children from divorced families do. I remember reading in a Sunday newspaper supplement about a celebrity divorce; the cover showed a young daughter saying, "Please come home, Daddy, and I will keep my room clean"—as if *that* might have contributed to his leaving.

In grammar school I was the only one in my class who did not have a father. Now that my sister has returned to teaching, she tells me horrifying stories of the decimation of the family unit. So many children are growing up full of anger and confusion and pain because of parental wars and split families.

There is such a need for the healing touch of Christ in our communities.

I see this struggle in the body of Christ. I see those who long to serve God with an undivided heart but their heart is broken. I see those who feel pulled in two, torn between the grace and mercy of God and the pain and cruelty of the world. Those of us who have gone through similar experiences can share some of the burden of our wounded brothers and sisters, but only Christ can fully know what any one soul is bearing. So we take the load to him.

Whatever you are carrying, take it to Jesus. That may sound simple and trite, but it is the very best choice that any of us can make. He who knelt in the garden and wept tears of blood, who had his body whipped and ripped on a wooden cross, understands the agony that tears at your soul. As he knelt in Gethsemene, facing the horror of what lay ahead, he prayed, "Father, if you are willing, take this cup from me; yet not my will, but yours be done" (Luke 22:42).

There is healing in the will of God, a pulling together of all the pieces of our lives. It doesn't mean that we will always understand what is happening to us, but we bring our torn edges to him who holds us together.

Lord,
There is so much pain in the world.
It leaves me speechless.
There is pain in my heart. It leaves me helpless.
I bring them both to you for you alone have carried the pain
of the world and the pain of your own heart.
In Jesus' name, Amen.

LOVE'S REVOLUTION

*Love is patient, love is kind. It does not envy, it does
not boast, it is not proud. It is not rude, it is not self-seeking,
it is not easily angered, it keeps no record of wrongs.*

1 CORINTHIANS 13:4

"What is holding you back?" I asked the young woman sitting beside me.

"I can't forgive and I can't forget, and it's tearing me apart," she said, tears pouring down her face.

"I don't expect that you will ever forget," I said. "But I believe that with God's help you can learn to forgive."

The details of her story were particular to her and yet her "I can't forgive" seemed so universal. I have said it myself and have heard it from many others. We feel as if our souls are being divided because we can't let go of what was and make peace with what is. We cry, "It's not fair," to the heavens. There is no immediate answer, because in a sense we're right: life is not fair and it never will be on this earth.

Life isn't fair. Does that mean we have to lug around this dead weight of disappointment until we get home? I don't believe so. Consider what Lewis Smedes says in his book *Forgive and Forget:* "Forgiving is love's revolution against love's unfairness. When we forgive we ignore the normal laws that strap us to the natural law of getting even, and by the alchemy of love we release ourselves from our own painful past."

God puts the power and the decision to forgive back into our hands. We can remain forever trapped by "what used to be," or by the marvelous grace of God we can choose to forgive—to bear no record of wrongs.

At some point in our lives we have to draw a line in the sand and let go of all the things that are holding us back, tearing our souls in two. Smedes calls it a revolution. That's a very fitting image—an overthrow of order and a new government. I don't want to spend the rest of my life reduced to keeping track of what was done to me. I think of the example that Christ left for us when he, the only innocent man who has ever lived, forgave freely from the cross. If any act perpetrated on a human being was unfair, surely it was Christ's crucifixion. And he will show us the way to let go of the wrongs against us. How can we stand at the foot of the cross and say to Christ, "It's not fair"? He hung on a tree for you and me—to give us a better way to live, to rise above the pain and the injustice of our world, to forgive as we have been forgiven. Welcome to the revolution!

Mismatched pieces, broken toys,
painful memories, girls and boys,
we bring them now to Calvary's tree
and leave them there for we are free.

Thank you, Lord, that because of your great gift we can forgive and we can live.

Amen.

CHEAP GRACE

When I kept silent, my bones wasted away through my groaning all day long. For day and night your hand was heavy upon me; my strength was sapped as in the heat of summer. Then I acknowledged my sin to you and did not cover up my iniquity. I said, "I will confess my transgressions to the LORD"—and you forgave the guilt of my sin.

PSALM 32:3–5

From upstairs she heard a noise of smashing glass. She called out to her son: "Are you all right, Sam? What happened?"

Little Sam's blond head appeared at the top of the stairs. "Sorry, Mom," he said. "I dropped my piggy bank and it broke."

"Oh, what a shame," she said. "You need to learn to be more careful, Sam. You always run at life."

Sam smiled sheepishly and disappeared into his room. He was very quiet that night at dinner.

"What's up, son?" his father asked. "Bad day at school?"

"No, Dad. Everything's fine."

"He dropped his piggy bank and it broke," his mother said.

"That's okay, Sam," his dad said. "We can get a new one."

His parents' words of comfort didn't seem to help Sam at all, and later that night when he was in bed, they heard him crying.

"Sam, whatever is the matter?" they asked as they sat on the edge of his bed. "We've forgiven you for smashing your piggy bank; it was an accident."

Through choked sobs Sam told them the whole truth. "It wasn't just my piggy bank," he explained. "I dropped it on Mom's crystal vase in your bedroom."

Sam had received no comfort from his parents' forgiveness because he had not faced the whole truth. He owned up to the smaller thing, but the full truth he held in his own heart. I believe that many of us feel divided in our souls because we have not faced all that is true about ourselves. Cheap grace is no grace at all. In *Letters and Papers from Prison,* Dietrich Bonhoeffer says that "It's the grace we bestow upon ourselves. Cheap grace is the preaching of forgiveness without requiring repentance."

To experience the grace of forgiveness and peace in our souls, we first have to deal with the bad news about ourselves. We have to face what our sin cost Christ; only in acknowledging that and repenting with a broken heart will the grace of God do its work in us as peace is restored to our souls. We can't gloss over our sins and skip to the good part as if it cost Christ so little. Such a surface work will bring only surface peace. True repentance brings true grace with all its depth and gifts.

> *The picture rolls before my eyes,*
> *the story of half truths and lies.*
> *I watch each frame with sorrow and with tears.*
> *But as the film rolls to an end,*
> *I see the screen washed clean again.*
> *He dries my eyes, a brand new show appears.*

Broken and Alive

Moreover, we have all had human fathers who disciplined us and we respected them for it. How much more should we submit to the Father of our spirits and live!

HEBREWS 12:9

Would you like to see the horses?" Bob, our host, asked. For a weekend Barry and I were staying on a horse ranch that stabled some of the most magnificent horses in America.

I am not very sure of myself around these huge powerful animals, but I said yes. As we walked toward the stables, memories of my last encounter with a horse came flooding back. I had been staying at a hotel in the English countryside. One morning I noticed a sign advertising gentle country walks on horseback. I signed up, thinking, "How hard can it be?" I asked the stable hand to give me a really old horse or one that could hardly walk. She gave me what she called a very gentle pony named Sam. It didn't look like a pony, it looked like King Kong.

We set off down a country lane. My horse had taken one look at me and sized me up immediately. He knew that I didn't have a clue as to how to handle him and that he was in charge. While everyone else was enjoying a nice quiet walk, my horse was eating entire trees. I ended up walking back for three miles, side by side with King Kong.

I came back from my reverie and our host was telling us that the ranch owners own the number-one homozygous horse in America. I asked what *that* meant. When bred, this stallion always produces Paint horses.

"Wait till you see his eyes," he said. We passed several magnificent animals and then stopped and gazed at this incredible stallion. His eyes were like fire, wild and intense. He was truly spectacular.

At dinner that evening I asked about the training these horses go through. What did "being broken" do to a horse? Did it break his spirit so that he was a only a shadow of himself?

"Until horses are broken, they are only consumers," Bob said. "When they are broken they are not less alive; they are more alive. It's as if they have found their purpose, what they were made for. There is such a unity then between horse and master. Wild horses might seem spectacular as they race across a canyon, but they are of no use to anyone but themselves. A horse that has been broken with love and respect is an animal in rhythm with its destiny."

That seemed such a perfect illustration of the process of being broken by Christ. In each of us there is a wild, unbroken being. How often I have cried out with the apostle Paul that the very thing that I don't want to do is the thing that I end up doing (see Romans 7). There is a part of me that wants nothing more than to please God, to do the things that honor him, to be loving and kind and merciful, but another part of me is selfish and arrogant. I don't know anyone who welcomes discipline, but it is God's direct answer to our prayers that he would heal our divided or torn souls. "No discipline seems pleasant at the time, but painful. Later on, however, it produces a harvest of righteousness and peace for those who have been trained by it" (Hebrews 12:11).

It's painful and it's hard work, and at times it's confusing, but when your will is finally submitted to God's will, there is a freedom that was never there before. There is a deep sense of destiny, of knowing why you were born and what you were made for.

There is nothing more stubborn than the human will. I have struggled for many years—torn between God's will and my own desires, but I am learning to trust the Master so that I am able by his grace to say, "Your will be done in every situation." I pray this not because I have given up hope, but because I have found the only One in whom my hope can rest.

Years ago that English "pony" looked at me and knew that I was not to be trusted as a master. But we follow the Master in whom complete and utter trust can be placed. So don't be discouraged by the discipline of the Lord; it will be the making of you.

Lord,
Thank you that you discipline me.
Thank you that this is a sign of your love for me.
Thank you that it shows your commitment to me.
Thank you that your discipline brings life.
In Jesus' name,

Amen.

PART EIGHT

RISK

The first requirement for growth in self understanding is an unswerving commitment to honesty with one's self. No one can break our chains for us, we have to do this for ourselves.

ELIZABETH O'CONNOR,
LETTERS TO SCATTERED PILGRIMS

*I*t was a beautiful old pocket watch. The little boy turned it over and over in his hands, polishing it on the edge of his sweater. He held it up to his ear and listened to the hypnotic ticktock melody of his most prized possession. He put it in his pocket and went home for dinner. That evening in bed he pulled it out from under his pillow. He held it tenderly up to the light and watched it spin on its chain.

"I wonder how it works?" he thought.

He slipped out of bed and listened at the door to hear if his mother and father were in bed. The house was quiet. He slipped out of his bedroom and downstairs. He turned on the kitchen light and took a small sharp knife from a drawer.

"I'll just open the back to see how it works," he reasoned. "I won't take anything out." He pried off the back of the watch and laid it facedown on the kitchen table. Inside he found an intricate maze of spinning, whirring, shiny metal. The temptation was too much. "I'll just take out a couple of things, to see what's underneath."

Soon it was all out on the table. He counted all the pieces and held them up to the light. *Sure is a mighty fine watch,* he thought. Before long he was sleepy and began to put the pieces back into the watchcase. They wouldn't fit. He tried again, in a different order. They didn't fit. He tried for an hour to put the delicate pieces of the watch back together, but no matter how hard he tried he could not get the pieces to fit into the watch casing. Large tears dropped on to his broken prize.

"Eddie, what's the matter?" his mother asked as she walked into the kitchen, tightening the belt on her bathrobe.

"I've ruined my watch," he sobbed. "I tried to see how it worked but I can't put it back together; it's ruined."

"It's not ruined, Eddie, but *we* can't fix it," his mother said. "We'll need to take it to a watchmaker."

"If you put the front piece back in, it looks okay, Mom," he said. "It still looks like a watch."

"But then it would be just a piece of jewelry. It was made for more than that."

You could wear a watch for years that looked pretty, but if it didn't work, it would be less than it was made for. So many people walk through their days with broken lives tidied up to look presentable—but not living as they were made to live. We were not made to be a piece of jewelry, decorative but barely functioning.

So where do you go when you can't fix your life? The only place to go is back to the One who made you. You have a divine destiny, a purpose from God that no one else can fulfill. It begins with a risk. We have to find the courage to take all the pieces of our lives, our hopes and dreams back to the One who made us—and ask him who we are. Then he, like the watchmaker, will carefully and gently replace our broken parts, showing us what we are meant to be and giving us all that we need to live our lives according to our purpose and his plan.

TO GROW WE HAVE TO RISK

In this way they will lay up treasure for themselves
as a firm foundation for the coming age, so that they may
take hold of the life that is truly life.

1 TIMOTHY 6:19

*D*avid sat at the bedside of a man whose breath was labored and shallow. The man stirred and opened his eyes. A nurse held a cup of water with a straw to the man's lips and then he turned his gaze to David, who introduced himself. "My name is David Pawson. I am chaplain here. Is there anything that I can do for you?"

The man stared at him and then laughed with energy he didn't have to spare. He coughed for a few moments.

"Shall I get the nurse?" David asked.

"No," the man replied. He looked at David intently. "Do you know who I am?"

Now David stared at him and said, "No, I am sorry; I don't recognize you. Have we met?"

"Hardly!" the man replied. "I am the president of the British Atheists Association.

"Do you want me to leave?" David asked.

"No. Stay awhile. I want to tell you why I don't believe in God."

David pulled his chair closer to the bed to make it easier for the man to speak.

"I don't believe in God because of you," he said bluntly.

"I don't understand," David responded. "Because of something I have done personally?"

"No," he replied. "Because of all of you. None of you believe what you say you believe."

"I still don't understand," David said.

The man pulled himself up in bed, and with all the energy and passion that was left to him, he looked directly into David's eyes. "If I believed what you all say that you believe, I would crawl over England on broken glass to tell people."

He sank back into his bed. The dialogue was over but those words of indictment were forever burned into the pastor's heart and soul.

Sometime later I met David at a conference. I was the singer and he was the guest speaker. As he told us this story, his voice caught when he related that dying man's final words to him; tears poured down David's cheeks. The words hung in the air. There was absolute silence in the room. We had spent almost an hour singing and rejoicing, celebrating God's love for us, but now the words of an atheist who spoke to us from the grave sobered us all. From the vantage point of the platform, I looked around the room and read the stories written on the faces in front of me. Some rolled their eyes as if to say, "What do you expect from a heathen?" Others shifted uncomfortably in their seats. Some were crying as they grasped the full impact of those words. I was devastated. I felt as shallow as a summer puddle after a short rain shower.

Think about it for a moment. We live in a desperate, decaying world, full of violence and hatred and fear. Every day teenagers take their lives because they see nothing to live for. In motel rooms all across our country, prostitutes give a little piece of their souls to men who don't even remember their faces. People drink and abuse drugs in an attempt to anesthetize their emotional pain and to try for a moment to stop thinking. We use and abuse each other in ways as old as our father Abraham. In the midst of all this chaos, there is a group of people, of whom I am one, who believe that there is hope written in letters as large as the Empire State Building: JESUS.

We know that there is more to this life than just getting through one more day. We actually believe that God loves us. We believe God's love was so intense that he sent his own Son to live among us—to show us what the Father is like and to die a brutal death in our place. We believe that whatever one's start in life, whatever mistakes one has made, there is forgiveness and a fresh start available. We believe that death is only the beginning of our real lives. We believe all of this, so why do we remain largely quiet about the good news?

I am not suggesting that we stand out on the street corner and wave banners in the faces of passersby. I am suggesting that we invite the Lord to deepen our understanding of his love, to stretch our hearts and fill us till we are running over with the grace and compassion of Christ. Then we would take risks. Then we would reach beyond ourselves—and *that* would stand out. That would be different. That would be real. That might even cause an atheist on his deathbed to find his way home.

Father God,
Forgive me for the apathy of my life.
Forgive me for clutching your words of life to my chest like a
life preserver
instead of throwing them out as a rope to the world.
Help me to live the words I believe,
to reach out beyond the comfort of my world,
to risk for you who risked all for me.

Amen.

RISKING EVERYTHING

Stand firm in the faith; be men of courage; be strong.
1 CORINTHIANS 16:13

*What matters is whether Christians will dare to risk
everything in order to fulfill their function in the world.*
JACQUES ELLUL,
THE PRESENCE OF THE KINGDOM

*T*he house was quiet now, but the raised voices of the men who
had carried her husband away still reverberated throughout the
room. It took her some time to settle her six children and reassure them that God would be with their father tonight.

But when will I be with him again? she asked herself.

They had known for some time that they were in danger.
Her husband, a dedicated pastor, had refused to bow to the Chinese authorities and surrender his house-church pulpit.

"How can I withhold the very words of life from those who
need to hear?" he had asked her.

For so long she had feared a night like tonight. With no
warning, a group of soldiers had burst into their quiet little
home, charged the pastor with crimes against the government,
and carried him away. It would be twenty-one years before she
would see her husband again. That was his sentence, twenty-one
years of hard labor in a prison miles from his family.

As she sat in the strange stillness of her room on that terrible night, she asked herself how she—alone—could possibly
support six children. A short time later, the authorities made her
an offer: If she would divorce and denounce her husband they
would take care of her and the children. She took a huge "risk"
and refused.

To take such a leap of faith, you need to know who you are and what you were made for. You need to be confident that you are in the loving hands of the all-powerful God.

My friend Marlene recently had an opportunity to interview this saintly Chinese woman. In their eighties, she and her husband are now reunited, living in China, preaching the Gospel. Marlene asked her if she had ever been angry with God during those twenty-one long years.

The woman laughed. "Ah yes," she said. "I was very angry for about two weeks, and then the Lord told me not to worry. He told me that he had need of my husband, because there were many in prison who had never heard about Christ. I knew then," she continued, "that if God was taking care of him in prison, he would take care of the children and me; and he did."

I am in awe of people like this who risk all they have to remain true to who they are.

Whether or not we are ever called to show such courage and fortitude, we, like this brother and sister, can know without a shadow of a doubt who we are and whose we are. Knowing that we can know why we are on this earth. That makes the rest of life fall into place — so that if we *are* called to take a stand for Christ—whether in a prison or an office building—our choice is made. We stand firm in our faith because it is our life.

Father God,
Today I lift up to you all those who suffer because they hold
your name up high. Give me the courage to hold my
standard strong whether in a howling gale or a gentle breeze.
In Jesus' name,

Amen.

OUT OF THE SHADOWS

Praise be to the God and Father of our Lord Jesus Christ, the Father of compassion and the God of all comfort, who comforts us in all our troubles, so that we can comfort those in any trouble with the comfort we ourselves have received from God.

2 CORINTHIANS 1:3–4

I must have just missed the call. I was out for only about twenty minutes taking Bentley for a run. When I returned I saw the familiar blink, blink on the answering machine and pressed the play button. "I just want to thank you for your book *Honestly*. I am a teacher who has been put on leave of absence and diagnosed with clinical depression. I felt so ashamed," the voice said. "I thought that I was the only one, you see. I didn't think that Christians suffered with this, and I felt so alone. I read your book, and I just want to say, God bless you for writing this. I know now that I'm not alone."

I listened to her voice and my heart went out to her. I said a prayer for her that God would be very close as she walks through this dark valley.

That call seemed important to the woman who left the message, but it also meant a lot to me. It brought home something that I strongly believe in. When I was considering writing *Honestly*, which dealt with my struggle with clinical depression, a couple of friends were concerned that some people would "not understand" and would dismiss me as some kind of nut, maybe pigeonhole me as the poster child for depression. I knew this was possible, but I also felt that we are called to take risks for one another, to stand beside those who are wounded, and to share the comfort we have received. There is such a stigma attached to any illness of the mind, and so many people suffer in silence, alone, afraid to admit that they are sinking a little more every day. I felt I should do what I could to break that silence and help others.

One particular occasion pushed me to write my story. I had been asked to speak at a women's prayer breakfast in Orange County, California. The organizing committee told me that I could talk about whatever was on my heart. I had never publicly talked about my hospitalization, and I hadn't arrived intending to do so. But as I looked out at that group of women, I felt moved to tell them where I had been and what God had done and was continuing to do in my life. As I talked I saw that tears streamed down many faces across the room. At the end of the morning I lingered and spoke with a few women who came up. I noticed a beautifully dressed woman hanging back a little, waiting for the crowd to thin out. Soon we were alone and we found a corner to sit and talk as the busboys cleared the tables.

"I haven't told anyone this," she said, "but I have suffered with depression for a year now. I have felt so ashamed and so alone. I cannot thank you ..." She could not continue, and we sat for a while holding hands, two sisters who have shared so many similar struggles. Her face stayed with me and I wondered how many others there were like her ... and so I wrote my book.

I used to be more concerned with being "inspirational" than with being real, but I now sense that people in pain need to know that they are not alone in their struggles; we need each other to be real. I am not advocating a coast-to-coast spiritual pity party, far from it. Rather, I suggest that as we receive the help and comfort of Christ, we in turn take a risk and extend that same hope and comfort to others. This is not a time to hide behind walls and put on a brave face; this is a time to stand in the light with our wounds and our flaws. Having taken that risk, we can encourage others to risk and come out of the shadows, find healing and find comfort in Christ. Those who reach out, who risk being known, will have the privilege of sharing the grace and mercy of God with others. (And believe me, there is a broken heart in every crowd.) That is what the family of God is all about.

> *Speak softly to the human heart*
> *that hides behind a wall.*
> *Speak words of life and comfort*
> *from the greatest gift of all.*
> *For every heart that's breaking*
> *needs a touch from Christ alone,*
> *so pour this oil*
> *on arid soil;*
> *speak softly to them all.*

YOU DID IT UNTO ME

The King will reply, "I tell you the truth, whatever you did for one of the least of these brothers of mine, you did for me."

MATTHEW 25:40

I loved her from the first minute I met her. Morag Gunn was one of a kind. She had a big heart and a crazy sense of humor, and I used to feel that she sometimes struggled with what other people expected of her. She was not what some would regard as the typical pastor's wife—stepping in to head up the women's ministry.

During my teenage years at Ayr Baptist Church, Edwin and Morag Gunn both had a tremendous impact on my life. Their house was always open to my best friend, Andree, and me. Then they were called to another church, in Glasgow, and I didn't get to see so much of them. My life moved on and I left home. When I was back, visiting my family, time was usually limited, and years went by before we were able to sit down together over a cup of tea and really catch up with each other.

"So how is life at Queens Park Baptist?" I asked Morag as she passed me a scone.

"I love it here," she said.

"Tell Sheila what you are doing now," Edwin encouraged.

As she told me about her new ministry, her face glowed. I recognized that look. It is the look of someone who has truly found her niche in the kingdom of God.

On weekends Morag and a couple of her friends leave their homes at eleven o'clock at night and head to the red-light district in Glasgow to minister to the prostitutes. "We take them a cup of tea and we just talk to them," she said. "It's heartbreaking to listen to some of their stories. The makeup doesn't cover their secrets. You can tell that some of them are no longer young and on a cold night they would rather be in a warm home sitting by a fire—but this is their life."

"Aren't you afraid out there, Morag?" I asked. "That's a pretty rough neighborhood."

"No, I'm not afraid," she replied. "They would stick up for me if there were any trouble, and I feel God's presence so close when I am with those women. I have found my place."

As I left and drove to Glasgow airport to catch my flight back home to Los Angeles, my heart was full of gratitude to God. Each one of us has a divine calling, a place to fill that no one else can. Sometimes we waste years trying to live out someone else's vision for our lives instead of finding what God has given us a heart for. It is a risky business to step out in new ways. We don't always receive the encouragement we would like, but that does not relinquish our responsibility to find out from God what we should be doing. I am so grateful that God does not squeeze us all into look-alike molds; he doesn't insist that we all care about the same things. Each one of us has a divine destiny, and when we discover that, we don't minister only to the world, we minister to the Lord.

> *I'm waiting in a quiet room.*
> *The crowds have all gone home.*
> *I'm standing by the door now.*
> *I had to come alone.*
> *I long to live the life that's mine,*
> *the one that bears my name,*
> *the one that's true—*
> *that comes from you*
> *and returns to you again.*
>
> *Amen.*

SATISFIED

As the deer pants for streams of water, so my soul pants for you, O God.

PSALM 42:1

I can't get no satisfaction."

The music blared from the banks of speakers at the Rose Bowl stadium. Seventy-eight thousand fans had packed the stadium for a Rolling Stones concert. Tucked away in a private box sat a group that didn't look like typical Rolling Stones fans. They were pastors and theologians who were attending the concert as part of a study on the impact of popular culture on society.

The president of the seminary I attend was one of these guests. Once I got over laughing at the thought of Dr. Mouw at a Stones concert, I was eager to hear his impressions of the evening.

"I looked at that vast crowd and realized that on Sunday, that many people would not attend all the churches in Pasadena," he said. "As I listened to the words of the song 'I can't get no satisfaction,' I thought of Psalm 42. We long in our souls for God and nothing else will do." He saw the universal thirst for God and he also identified a second human longing. "When I looked at these people dancing together, familiar with the words to every song, I realized that for a few moments they were fulfilling that great need for community, that longing to belong to something, to be part of something."

As I thought about what Dr. Mouw said, I went through the stack of poems I have written over the last few years and found what I was looking for.

And all my life I've been afraid of letting people in,
of giving them the power to wound,
to take my ship and watch it run aground.
So help me, Lord, unclench my fists,
throw open shuttered doors,
and in this dance,
this fine romance,
the fragrance will be yours.

The whole world stands with one song on its lips. It is a song that reflects our deep hunger, our thirst for something more. But it's scary to reach out to others and be open and vulnerable, and to ask for help, because of the great potential for being hurt. Even as Christians we are afraid at times to let go and let God into the deepest places of our hearts. As the people of God, it's time to take a risk. It's time to reach out to God and to one another and be open and available. . .

For there are depths of love we'll never know
until we've given everything we've got
and found that we are richer than we ever dreamed
and safer, so much safer, than we thought.

PART NINE

NIGHT

Oh Lord my God, when the storm is loud, and the night is dark, and the soul is sad, and the heart oppressed; then, as a weary traveler, may I look to you; and beholding the light of your love, may it bear me on, until I learn to sing your song in the night.

GEORGE DAWSON,
LITTLE BOOK OF PRAYERS

𝒫lay something, Mom," I urged, as my mother rested in her chair after dinner.

"What do you want to hear?" she asked.

"Some of the songs from the old *Redemption Hymnal*," I said. In our church back home we used the *Baptist Hymnbook* on Sunday mornings and the *Redemption Hymnal* at night. Its old gospel songs of faith and hope, such as "We're Marching to Zion" and "Standing on the Promises," were some of my favorites.

Mom pulled her weary bones out of the chair and walked slowly to the piano. I love to hear her play. And as she began, my sister and I sang along. The music filled the room with warmth and melody.

My mom has an unusual style of piano playing. She uses only the black keys. One day as a kid I asked her, "Why do you play only on the black notes?" I had started piano lessons at school, and I knew that this was not the correct way.

"I taught myself to play when I was a child," she said. "I play by ear, and this is the only way I can do it."

It was a familiar sound to me and I loved it, but I realized sometime later that our old piano was capable of so much more. My sister, Frances, dated a boy from school, and one night when he was over for dinner he sat down at the piano and played. When Ian used all the keys, the piano sounded like a different instrument. The depth and dimension of sound that came out of "old faithful" amazed me. It sounded so complete.

Suffering and sorrow are never welcome guests. They take us by surprise and squeeze our hearts, but I believe they are necessary to make the melody of our lives complete. It's possible to try to live your life in one color, protecting yourself from the full spectrum of human experience, but the sounds that emerge are a little hollow and one-dimensional.

We were made for the joy and laughter of the major keys and also for the pain and tears of the minor. Part of being fully alive to God is being willing to embrace all that he puts in our path. That includes the unexpected stones that scrape our souls, so that we can become more like him.

When I study the life of Christ, I sense a deep, rich symphony ascending to the heart of God—using every note and inflection. This is what we, too, were made for.

God Is Awake

He will not let your foot slip—he who watches over you will not slumber.

Psalm 121:3

Have courage for the great sorrows of life and patience for the small ones. And when you have finished your daily task, go to sleep in peace. God is awake.

Victor Hugo

*M*ost days I am happy to be alive. Many days drift along in sameness. But sometimes there are days like today when my heart is heavy and sad; I have a dear friend who is in trouble.

From the day she was born it seemed as if the nails were driven into her soul. Her birth mother and father decided not to raise her; she was surrendered for adoption. That would be a gift for some who find love and a real family in the loving arms of people who have prayed for such a miracle. But the home she was placed into was not a safe place. She was sexually and physically abused from the age of five, and in her early teens she turned to prostitution and a life on the streets.

There, for the first time, she had family. The other kids on the streets took her in and cared for her. She found a place to belong. Drugs and alcohol took some of the edge off the filth and some of the cold out of the nights.

One day a girl walked up to her and asked if she knew that Jesus loved her. She laughed. Amidst the abuse, her adoptive mother had preached to her about adhering to the laws of the Bible—if she didn't, her mother said, she would roast in hell. But something in her cried out to believe that somewhere there could be a God who loved her. So she wandered into a church and prayed to be accepted into God's family. It wasn't easy to break away from the life she had known. It wasn't easy to walk away from her street family, particularly since everyone in her new Christian family seemed so busy, but she had courage and she set her face to loving God.

We've known each other for about seven years. She wrote to me when I was co-host of "The 700 Club," and over time we became good friends. I need her in my life. She is honest and kind, and she tells me when I am full of hot air.

Life has not become any easier for her. She has life-threatening health problems. She has been institutionalized for depression in a state hospital, where they kept her so doped up that she was like a vegetable. Through it all she has tried so hard to keep living for Christ.

Today she told me that she can't do it anymore. As one disaster follows another, she is tired of trying to be hopeful about her life. She wants to end it now. She is not trying to manipulate me or make me feel sorry for her. She is just being herself, telling me the truth: "I can't take this anymore." We talked for an hour and she promised me that she would not do anything today.

I called her tonight; she is being admitted to a state mental hospital on a "seventy-two-hour hold." When she had to hang up because the hospital attendant was there to pick her up, I felt so desperate, so angry. I don't understand why her life has to be like this. Why is it that some people find flowers wherever they turn, and others are stung every time they reach out their hands? We prayed together on the phone, tears pouring down our faces. I know that she is afraid. She has told me before that she would rather die than go back to one of those places.

I read that despair cuts us off from mercy. But sometimes mercy seems so slow to come. I know that we are promised that we will not be given more than we can bear. But I look at my friend and that doesn't seem true. I have such an ache in my soul that I don't know what to do with myself. So I sit here at my computer and write until I can go and see her. I walk around my house and I cry out to God. I remind him in my broken arrogance of all the things that he has promised. I tell him, as if he has forgotten, that he has a very scared daughter who is locked away tonight, who needs him. And even as I write I am reminded that my ache for my friend does not hold a candle to the relentless compassion of Christ. They won't let me into her ward tonight, but they can't keep him out.

When emotions beat against our souls like wave after wave in the worst of a storm, there is nowhere to turn but to Christ. As I sit for a while and think about him, I hear the loneliest words in the world: "Jesus cried out in a loud voice, *'Eloi, Eloi, lama sabachthani?'*—which means, 'My God, my God, why have you forsaken me?'" (Matthew 27:46). On that brutal tree Christ embraced total isolation so that you and I never have to be alone. I am learning that that doesn't mean that life will be free of pain; it means that in the midst of the darkest night, he comes walking. Along the bleakest hospital corridors, he comes walking. When you think that the world has left you all alone, listen closely, he comes walking.

> *I lie here in the darkness.*
> *The walls are closing in,*
> *when morning seems a world away*
> *and all the fears begin.*
> *I call upon you, Jesus, to walk me through this night,*
> *and peace will fall within these walls,*
> *my Savior and my light.*
>
> *Amen.*

THE GIFT OF CRISIS

A certain ruler asked him, "Good teacher, what must I do to inherit eternal life?" . . .

[Jesus] said to him, "You still lack one thing. Sell everything you have and give to the poor, and you will have treasure in heaven. Then come, follow me."

When he heard this, he became very sad, because he was a man of great wealth.

LUKE 18:18, 22–23

I love to listen to audio books. If I have a long drive the miles seem to melt away as Garrison Keillor takes me to Lake Wobegon or Meryl Streep reads *The Velveteen Rabbit*. On this particular day I had received a package of tapes in the mail from Pastor Bob Phillips.

I stopped at my usual coffee haunt for a cup of latte—to go—and put the first tape in the cassette player in my car. The message was about the young successful man who stopped to talk to Jesus to check that his spiritual life was as on track as his business portfolio.

The man didn't receive the answer he was hoping for. In fact he was told to take everything that was working for him and get rid of it, to strip himself of his very identity as a wealthy man. He was obviously a good man, a decent citizen. Why then was he asked to reduce himself to the ranks of the poor and destitute?

I used to puzzle over this story. Jesus must have encountered many wealthy people without requiring that they give everything away. Even Zacchaeus, who had cheated people all of his life, gave only half of his wealth to the poor (Luke 19:8). So why was Christ so hard on this man?

As I listened, Bob said something that made me turn off the tape and think for a long time. It was one of those *Eureka!*

moments, when you know that what you just heard is very important. Bob said that Jesus created a crisis in this man's life to show the man what was within him. It really had nothing to do with the money per se; it's just that money was in this man's heart as an idol. With that insight the gospel story made sense.

What Christ cares about is our hearts, our complete love and devotion. And he will create crisis in our lives to show us what holds us.

I remember how devastated I was when I found myself in a psychiatric ward, suffering from clinical depression, with a career lying in tatters at my feet. At first glance my situation looked like the worst thing that could ever happen to me. But that was just the first look.

As I looked closer I began, slowly, to see that I had been given the most awesome gift, the gift of crisis, to see what was in my soul. Some of it was ugly. I saw fear and anger, pride and unforgiveness, but I also saw Christ there with open arms, inviting me to change. What a gift!

We don't need to view crisis as an enemy but as a friend. If we see that the whole purpose of life is to become more like Jesus, then crisis is indeed a gift, for as the weeds of our hearts are exposed, they can be uprooted. That is painful sometimes, but pain is very necessary if we want to grow.

The gospel account of the "rich young ruler" ends by saying that he went away sad and that Christ let him go. Jesus didn't run after him and say, "Okay, how about fifty percent?" Jesus let him walk away. What God is after in the darkest night of our souls is our whole heart, nothing less. If you find yourself in the midst of a crisis, stop for a moment and thank God, invite him into the crisis, and see what he will make of you.

Dear Lord,
Thank you that you love me enough to gift me with crisis.
I pray for courage that I will not fall back.
I pray for grace that I will not give in.
I pray for eyes to see you in the darkest moments of my life.

Amen.

COMFORT

*For just as the sufferings of Christ flow over into our
lives, so also through Christ our comfort overflows.*

2 CORINTHIANS 1:5

*I*n my hotel room I unpacked my case quickly and hung my suit
for the next day's conference. I changed my watch from California to Detroit time and called Debbie.

"Hi, I'm here. Are you up for a visit?" I asked her.

"Are you kidding!" she replied. "Get yourself over here, now!"

I called down to the front desk and asked for a cab. As I
rode about fifteen minutes over to my friend's house, I wondered
what I would see when I got there. Debbie had tried to warn me
that she did not look good and had deteriorated considerably
since my last visit. I knew that the flesh on her right leg was all
but gone, not only from the cancer, but also from the flesh-
eating virus she had caught. I prayed, "Lord, please help me to
be strong for Debbie." Since I was pregnant, my stomach was
unreliable. Sometimes just fixing the dog's breakfast was enough
to make me lose mine.

"Here we are, Miss," the cab driver said.

Debbie's mom, Mildred, was at the front door, a smile
warming up her tired face. We hugged each other and com-
mented on how long it had been since we had last been together.
Debbie's dad shook my hand. As I hugged her two sisters I could
see my friend out of the corner of my eye, sitting in a wheelchair
in the family den. I walked over and gave her a very gentle hug.
Her right arm is broken but they can't put it in a cast because the
extra weight would break her fragile shoulder.

"Hi, friend!" I said, as she grinned up at me.

"Well, you don't look very pregnant!" she said in mock indignation. "I thought you'd look like Shamu by now!"

"Any day now," I reassured her.

The family gathered round to share a pizza, and we caught up on each other's news. Then, as if by some unspoken signal, they all drifted off and left Debbie and me alone.

"So how are you really doing?" I asked.

"Not so good," she said. "I'm so tired. I don't think I can do this much longer. The pain never leaves and having the dressings changed on my wounds is more than I can bear. The cancer is spreading to new areas. I really don't know how I'm still alive."

I looked at my friend, wrapped in a decimated sixty-five-pound body, and I too did not know how it was possible that she was still alive. For years she has struggled. Of all the people I have encountered in my life, I know of no one who has suffered more than Debbie.

"How is this affecting your faith, Debbie?" I asked.

She sat for a moment in silence and then replied.

"I've actually lost a lot of faith," she told me, "faith in the things of this world. I've lost faith in all the silly things that we think are so important, all the stuff we do to impress each other, but my faith in Christ is stronger than ever."

"Help me understand that," I countered. "When you are in so much pain, where is Christ?"

"When I am rushed to the hospital again and I can't breathe and I'm bleeding internally and all around me is panic—at those moments it is as if Christ gathers me up into his arms and holds me. He is the only one who can hold me and not break anything."

I looked at my dear friend and knew that this was no Pollyanna. She was confirming what Paul told us: "Just as the sufferings of Christ flow over into our lives, so also through Christ our comfort overflows."

Debbie has asked me to conduct her funeral service, and I consider it to be one of the highest honors I could ever be given. It will not be a time of wailing for the end of something but a time of celebration for the homecoming of a saint of God who, in the darkest night of her life, held on to Jesus as he held on to her.

Her footprints are fewer than mine,
every one is executed at a high price;
some hardly make a mark,
like a feather descending onto snow.
But if you stop for a moment and look at where they're going
their path is very clear:
They're going home,
a straight line home.
You're almost home, my dear.

Amen.

WAITING IN THE DARK

He went away a second time and prayed, "My Father, if it is not possible for this cup to be taken away unless I drink it, may your will be done."

MATTHEW 26:42

I had never been angry with God. I'd found it hard to relate to others who had told me they struggled with this; it seemed so foreign to me—until recently. I was doing well in my pregnancy. Because I turned forty in my fourth month, I knew I was considered higher risk than some women, but I didn't give it much thought.

Based on intuition and guesswork, we were sure it was a girl and had chosen a name, Alexandra Elizabeth.

"Are you disappointed that it's not a boy?" I asked my husband.

"Absolutely not!" he said. "I just want a healthy baby."

At nineteen weeks I went for an ultrasound. Barry took the day off work, and we were so excited we didn't know what to do with ourselves. "Well, do you want to know the sex?" the nurse asked.

"Yeah, we'd love to!" we replied in unison.

"It's a healthy-looking boy."

I thought that Barry was going to hit his head on the ceiling. He let out a yell of delight and did some thanksgiving dance known only to men.

"I guess he's happy!" the nurse said, smiling at me. We left the hospital on cloud nine. I did a quick mental switch and realized that I was going to love being mom to a little boy; I'm not the froo-froo lace and ribbons type. We stopped on the way home and bought him five outfits and then called our families and shared our joy with them.

Two days later my doctor called. "Are you sitting down?" she said.

"Yes," I said. "What's wrong?"

"Your blood screening test came back and it doesn't look good," she explained. "I'd like to have you meet with a genetic counselor as soon as possible."

I knew what she was talking about. This was a test that screened for birth defects and was given routinely to women over thirty-five. I called Barry at work. He took the morning off and came with me. We walked into that waiting room as one sober couple. We didn't talk. We sat and held hands until they called my name. The counselor brought out charts and graphs and talked on and on, but I couldn't hear him. All I could hear was that something was wrong with our baby.

"I've made an appointment for you to have an amniocentesis at eleven o'clock," he said.

"Why would I do that?" I asked. "We're not going to abort the baby, no matter what the problem is."

"Well, that's your choice," he said. "But if the baby is very handicapped and your doctor knows that information, it will help in the delivery."

"How long will we have to wait for the results?" Barry asked.

"Ten days," he said.

Later, waiting for the test, I lay on the table with none of the joy that I had felt a few days ago. The nurse brought the baby's picture onto the screen so the doctor would not harm him when he put the needle into the amniotic sac. I looked at this little one wriggling around, full of life, and I had to turn my head away from Barry as the tears flowed down my face.

"This will hurt a little," the doctor said as he pushed the needle in and extracted two vials of fluid.

"Honey, whatever happens, the Lord will be with us, and I will be beside you every step of the way."

I looked at my husband and smiled, but inside I was a cauldron of emotions.

"Why don't you lie down for a while?" Barry said when we got home.

"The timing of this could not be worse," I said. I was leaving the next morning for a ten-day tour to promote my book *Honestly*. Barry would not be with me on the trip, so we would have to wait separately, me in Dallas and Barry at home.

For the first two days on the road, I was okay. I cried at times, but that seemed to give me some relief. Then an unfamiliar emotion surfaced, and I realized that I was angry at God.

"If this is supposed to be another test to make me a better Christian, then forget it. I don't want it that badly," I cried. "I'll stay the way I am."

I felt torn in two. I couldn't deny what I was feeling, and yet I felt ashamed of what I was feeling. What right did I have to demand a "perfect" child? And yet I wanted to make that demand. The waiting seemed the hardest part.

I imagined what life would be like, raising a handicapped child. "You're a hypocrite, Sheila," I told myself. "You tell people that the handicapped kids you used to work with were some of the most loving people you've ever known. You just don't want one of your own."

I didn't want to talk to God; I knew that I had to make my peace with him about whatever was going to happen, but I didn't want to.

This struggle went on for a week. Then, on the seventh day, I was in Marion, Illinois, for a TV interview. By early afternoon it was over. I didn't know what to do with myself, so I decided to catch a movie. And the only theater in town was showing *Jack*. The movie, starring Robin Williams, was about a baby born with a birth defect that causes him to grow at four times the normal rate. I almost left the theater, but something about it made me stay. I watched the parents agonize over Jack's safety, the ridicule of other kids. I saw this man-child, ten years old but looking forty, live life with all he had. His courage and strength and struggle and tears changed everyone around him.

I drove back to the Holiday Inn and got down beside my bed.

"This is all right," I prayed. "We can do this together. I accept whatever is ahead, knowing that it will be part of the great adventure. Thank you for letting me be angry; thank you for staying by my side."

> *Kneeling in a garden, weeping on your own,*
> *longing for the play to change,*
> *a rewrite for a tomb,*
> *choosing in the darkness to play it to the end.*
> *I come to you*
> *who surely knows how hard it is to bend.*
> *But bend I will into this wind*
> *no matter how I ache*
> *and trust that in the worst of times*
> *you will not let me break.*
> *I get up off this dusty floor and set my course for home,*
> *safe in the truth: I'm not alone*
> *because you faced your tomb.*

Postscript: That evening Barry called me with the news that the test results had come back early, indicating "no problem."

PUSHING THROUGH
THE NIGHT

You need to persevere so that when you have done the will of God, you will receive what he has promised.
HEBREWS 10:36

I inherited my love of books and reading from my mother, an avid reader. When I think of my childhood home, there's always a book by Mom's chair. She taught us to treat books with respect and care; after all, they introduced us to other worlds and experiences.

Her bookshelves were lined with the works of Charles Dickens (*David Copperfield* being the favorite) and great works of the faith. And Mother loved the writings of A. J. Cronin. Until the age of thirty-three, Cronin was a doctor in London. Then due to poor health, he quit his practice and moved to a quiet little village in Scotland. He decided to try his hand as an author.

Like most worthwhile pursuits, writing was not easy. Cronin quickly became discouraged, convinced that what he had managed to commit to paper was worthless. Surely he had been fooling himself to imagine that he could write something of value. In despair he left his desk and went for a walk. In the countryside he encountered Angus, an old farmer patiently working the harsh peat. In a *Reader's Digest* article he recalls that conversation, him telling the old man that he was quitting as a writer.

The farmer listened and then said, "No doubt you're the one that's right and I'm the one that's wrong. But I've been working this bog all my days and never made a pasture of it. But pasture or no pasture I canna help but dig, for my father knew and I know that if you only dig for long enough a pasture can be made here."

That simple declaration of purpose was a turning point in Cronin's life. He went back to his desk and continued to work on the book that became *Hatter's Castle,* which sold more than three million copies and was translated into nineteen languages. The greatest victory here was that Cronin overcame himself and his self-doubt. As Shakespeare said, "Our doubts are traitors."

As a child of God, each of us has a divine call and destiny, and yet so often we are held back by fear and doubt. We are afraid of making a mistake, of looking foolish. We find it easy to believe that God can use someone else. But us? It requires a leap of faith to grasp hold of the truth that God can take us beyond our own abilities; we must simply trust him and keep pushing on through the night. The Word of God never says we mustn't make a mistake, but it has a lot to say about those who doubt. There's James 1:6, for example: "But when he asks, he must believe and not doubt, because he who doubts is like a wave of the sea, blown and tossed by the wind."

It is easy to believe that God can use our lives when we see immediate results, when positive feedback encourages us to push on. It is hard to keep walking when we see little sign that what we are doing is making a difference. I think of that farmer plowing away by the loch, knowing that what he was doing would one day make a difference. Perhaps he never saw it himself, perhaps his son or grandson finally gleaned the fruit of their labor—but a pasture was there.

Perhaps there is little immediate satisfaction in what you have been called to do, but if you will faithfully push on through the night the Lord is the one who carries a reward in his hands.

The earth seems dry and barren, Lord.
The wind is in my face.
I think of laying down these tools
to find a better place,
and yet there's something in this soil that calls to me to stay
and follow through, to follow you, to walk until it's day.

Amen.

PART TEN

WORSHIP

*And so the yearning strong, with which the soul
   will long,*
Shall far out-pass the power of human telling;
No soul can guess his grace, till it becomes the place
Wherein the Holy Spirit makes his dwelling.
                               BIANCO DA SIENA

*I*t was a perfect spring day as I climbed the steps to Sacre Coeur, the most beautiful church in Paris. Set in the Montmartre area of the city, it is surrounded by cobbled streets, quaint little restaurants, and a cluster of local artists. I stopped at the top of the stairs to catch my breath and to let a group of excited tourists come tumbling out of the sanctuary.

I had visited the Cathedral of Notre Dame the day before. I had admired its beauty, the magnificent stained-glass windows, the stone pillars that reached to the sky, but I was not prepared for this experience. As I entered the church there were two paths to follow. One led around the perimeter, where, as a tourist, I could admire the splendor of the building. The other welcomed me to take a seat close to the altar as a worshiper.

I quietly sat down and bowed my head to pray. I've visited many of the world's most famous and brilliant edifices, but I've never felt such a keen perception of the holiness of God. All around me tourists pointed to particular details illustrated in their guidebooks, but the greatest gift of all seemed to go largely unnoticed. I was overwhelmed by the sense of God's presence in this place. I turned to look at my mother who was traveling with me. Her cheeks were wet with tears. In the midst of a busy, fascinating city, we had found a place to rest and be alone with God.

I have often wondered what it was about that particular place that evoked such intimacy with God in the midst of a crowd. It wasn't the beauty of the building or the colors of the stained-glass windows; it was as if God was pleased to meet with us there. Perhaps the hands that built the Sacre Coeur soaked it in prayer. Maybe the church staff makes a daily request to God that those who seek him will find him there. It felt like a place that was prepared and ready; though it lent itself to different uses, it existed for only one thing—to welcome the presence of God.

We were created for one thing, to be a temple for the living God. As I think of my life as a house of worship, that is what I pray: that I will welcome the presence of God. It is a struggle to me at times, and maybe it is for you, too. There are so many demands put on our time and gifts. Just as it would be possible to spend time in this beautiful church and never meet with God, never be quiet, never listen, so in my own life it is easy to rush around enjoying the architecture of life, or even maintaining my life as a building, and ignoring the purpose of the building. We are not tourists in this world; we are people with a purpose and a calling.

A HUMBLE HEART

Lord, if you are willing, you can make me clean.
MATTHEW 8:2

I didn't expect it to be so beautiful. When I think of Texas, I think of big cities, huge cattle ranches, and steaks the size of Omaha. This was different.

Barry and I had flown to San Antonio and picked up a rental car to drive to a small town called Kerrville. I had been invited by Pastor Del Way of Calvary Temple to sing a couple of songs in the Sunday morning service and give an evening concert. The closer we got to our destination the more picturesque the scenery became. Rolling hills and green fields stretched out before us for miles.

"I could live here," I said.

"Me too," Barry replied.

"We could have five dogs and two horses and chickens and maybe a goat or two," I suggested.

"You and one dog and one cat is more than enough for me!" he said with a grin.

We arrived at our hotel and unpacked. We slept like babies and woke refreshed the next morning. As I sat in the church service I was moved by the atmosphere of worship. Even the teenage boys were singing with all their hearts. *This is a special place,* I thought.

After my last song Del got up to speak. His message was simple and startling to me. Like so many of the most powerful truths in the world, the kernel was simple truth. His message was taken from Matthew's gospel, a story I have known since childhood, and yet I heard it that day as if the ink were not yet dry on the manuscript.

A man with leprosy came and knelt before him and said, "Lord, if you are willing, you can make me clean."
Jesus reached out his hand and touched the man. "I am willing," he said. "Be clean!" Immediately he was cured of his leprosy. *Matthew 8:2–3*

Matthew says that multitudes were following Jesus wherever he went, but there was something different about this man, even apart from his leprosy. The Greek word used here for *knelt* is from the root "to worship," to kneel down and lick someone's hand like a dog, in total humility. I'm sure that there were many needs present in the crowd that day, but the one who received his miracle was the man who humbled himself and knelt at the feet of Christ and worshiped, saying, "If you are willing, you can make me clean."

In bed that night I thought about that for a long time. How can we appropriate the faith and humility of this man? So many of us go to great lengths to follow the "latest move" of God. We make sure we attend the right conventions and read all the right books; we are "with Christ," part of the "in" crowd. But I think God asks us simply to fall at his feet and worship, to acknowledge that we cannot heal ourselves, that we are dependent on him every moment. Going deeper in our lives with God is a more solitary life. I am committed to community. It is the church, it is our calling, but it is only as we are real with God and broken before him that we have anything to bring to one another.

I used to try and find a perfect formula to worship at home. I would get out a hymnbook and sing my way through many of the great hymns of the faith. Or I would work with a book of liturgy. I would sing worship choruses until my cat hid under the bed, but the formulas were barren to me until I began literally to prostrate myself on the floor before the Lord, confessing my weakness and sinfulness. Now as I meditate on the goodness of God, I find myself singing or weeping or laughing. Worshiping God.

I have no ten steps to offer you, but I do encourage you to follow the lead of a leper and fall at the feet of Jesus and worship him. We are called to be a home for God, a prepared room where he can live and pour out his life and love.

> *Falling at your feet I throw my life into your care.*
> *I worship at your feet; my heart has found a true*
>   *home there.*
> *Nothing in my hands I bring,*
> *my life my only offering.*
> *My heart in broken gladness sings*
> *That Christ has met me here.*

COMMITTED TO WORSHIP

Worship the LORD with gladness; come before him
with joyful song.

PSALM 100:2

[The word] cells, as the monks call their rooms, has
nothing to do with prison cells. Cell comes from the Latin
word cella, *related to the word* coelum, *heaven, the place*
where one enjoys God.

BASIL PENNINGTON,
A PLACE APART

I have enjoyed the presence of God in all sorts of places. Whether walking over the green hills of Scotland or down by the ocean as the waves crash over my feet, there is something about the beauty of God's creation that welcomes praise and worship, calls it from my soul.

But what about the dark days? What about the days when you are cut off from anything of beauty? Perhaps no one understands that better than Pastor Ha. He now lives with his wife and two children just a few miles from where I used to live in southern California, but he used to be the pastor of the largest church in Saigon. During some very difficult days for the church, he was imprisoned for six years, including sixteen months in solitary confinement. The prison was a dank, miserable hole. How do you worship in a place like that? What is there in your surroundings that would remind you of the goodness of God? Pastor Ha is a very unusual man. He discovered that if he put his head down the toilet in his solitary cell, he could preach to the prisoners in the cells below; he sang hymns of praise to encourage them and bring some comfort into their darkness.

Can you imagine such a thing? I have such a strong image of this godly man down on his hands and knees with his head down a toilet bringing words of life to dying men as he worshiped God, his life a testimony to his love for and devotion to Christ. I hear him singing:

> *Great is Thy faithfulness, O God my Father,*
> *There is no shadow of turning with Thee;*
> *Thou changest not, Thy compassions, they fail not;*
> *As Thou hast been Thou forever wilt be.*
> *Great is Thy faithfulness! Great is Thy faithfulness!*
> *Morning by morning new mercies I see;*
> *All I have needed Thy hand hath provided—*
> *Great is Thy faithfulness, Lord, unto me.*
>
> THOMAS CHISHOLM

Worship is a call. It is not a pat on God's back for giving us a good day or an answer to a particular prayer. Perhaps you find yourself in circumstances that are less than inspirational. As you look around at your life, you are disappointed with what you see. I ask you for a moment to think about our brother locked away from his wife and family—in a miserable jail cell with his head down a toilet, worshiping God. Remember that we worship God not because he has strewn our lives with a Christmas list of gifts but because he is God; he is our God and he is worthy to be praised.

> *Great is Thy faithfulness! Great is Thy faithfulness!*
> *Morning by morning new mercies I see;*
> *All I have needed Thy hand hath provided—*
> *Great is Thy faithfulness, Lord, unto me.*

A ROYAL INVITATION

> *But you are a chosen people, a royal priesthood, a holy nation, a people belonging to God, that you may declare the praises of him who called you out of darkness into his wonderful light.*

1 PETER 2:9

I started off by myself at nine o'clock in the morning. I figured I would break for lunch at twelve-thirty and keep going until the stores closed at five. What do you wear to meet a princess?

In two weeks I was to co-host a Royal Gala concert at the Royal Albert Hall in London for Save the Children Fund. Princess Anne was the patron of this charity and would be present in the royal box. My co-host and I would be presented to the princess at the end of the evening. I tried on dress after dress. Too stuffy. Too expensive. Too frilly. Too tight.

Eventually, as the sun was beginning to set, I found a dress I liked and flopped down in Harrod's tearoom for a much-needed cup of tea. I went over the instructions that my co-host, British rock star Alvin Stardust, and I had received from the palace. It was made very clear that there was a right way and a wrong way to address royalty. When the princess was first introduced to us, we were to refer to her as "Your Royal Highness." After that, we could call her "Ma'am." The previous evening, at home in front of my mirror, I had practiced curtsying, and the best I could do looked more like fainting than curtsying.

The evening was a huge success. The Royal Albert Hall is one of the most beautiful concert venues in Europe, and on that night it sparkled. The British Broadcasting Company televised the event. When the last encore was taken and the stage lights went down, it was time to be presented to the princess.

I stood in line beside Alvin and waited. Suddenly there was a commotion and the royal party approached. As I watched the elegant princess walk toward me, my mind went completely blank. *What do I call her?* I racked my brain, but I could not remember. *Is it "Your Majesty"? . . . No, that's the Queen . . . Is it . . . ?*

Suddenly I heard a man's voice. "This is one of tonight's presenters, Miss Sheila Walsh."

I looked at Princess Anne and said the only thing that came to my mind: "Hello!"

People have been beheaded for less!

She was very gracious, however. She smiled and shook my hand, telling me how much she had enjoyed the evening. As she moved along the line, Alvin Stardust glared at me as if I were a terrorist.

In Britain you are raised to hold the royal family in a place of great respect and honor. You never speak unless you are spoken to; you bow or curtsy when you are introduced; and when they move on, the conversation is over.

Earthly royalty should be honored and treated with respect but their rule is limited to this earth; their kingdom is not eternal. Our God is a majestic ruler who would only have to speak a word and every throne would crumble, every earthly power be diminished. It is so amazing then to think that we who trust in Christ have access through his blood to the very throne room of heaven itself. What a gift through the sacrifice of Christ.

I spent so much time getting ready for my "big day" in London, but so often I enter carelessly into the presence of the King of Kings. God is our Father, so we enter his presence with confidence through Christ. We don't have to prepare and remember the perfect greeting. Read the psalms and you can see that. But it's easy to forget that God is also the Lord of the universe. Let us enter with reverent worship.

> *Holy, Holy, Holy!*
> *Though the darkness hide thee,*
> *Though the eye of sinful man*
> *Thy glory may not see,*
> *Only thou art holy;*
> *There is none beside thee*
> *Perfect in power, in love, and purity.*
>
> REGINALD HEBER

SPECIAL MOMENTS

Glorify the LORD with me; let us exalt his name together.

PSALM 34:3

I had one of those moments today. I was standing in the kitchen as the sun was setting behind the hills. Lights were beginning to dot the hillside, and the temperature was dropping to a comfortable place. Bentley was in the yard, lying peacefully by the flower beds, eating a bone, and I could hear Barry singing in the shower. I looked across the kitchen into the den and my eyes rested on the navy blue stroller we have purchased for our son. Since it has no human occupant at the moment, we have placed our old teddy bears inside.

I put the kettle on to boil water for tea. As I opened the refrigerator to get the milk, I stopped to look at the photographs that grace the door. There is one of Bentley as a puppy; he's looking a little lost and wears a big green ribbon round his neck. There is one of my mother and my aunt Mary, who, at eighty, still lives by herself in a village just outside my hometown. There is a picture of my brother, Stephen, holding his son who will be a year old when our boy is born. Stephen holds him with such tenderness; as I think back to playing football in the yard and climbing trees together, it hardly seems possible that my little brother is a daddy. Then my eyes turn to a picture of Billy and Ruth Graham at home in North Carolina, books scattered everywhere, reflecting Ruth's passion for reading. There is a picture of my family gathered together last Christmas, everyone wearing silly party hats at my insistence.

During this brief reverie I heard no traffic noise or dogs barking; it was as if for a moment all the world was at peace. Suddenly I felt as if my heart was overflowing with praise to God for his goodness to me. I was surrounded by all the things that remind me of the grace and mercy of the Lord. I felt the baby kick and went to join Bentley in the evening air.

I prayed, "Lord, there are no words that could even begin to thank you for all you have done for me. I feel as if I am the richest woman on the planet. I pray for this little one moving inside of me that he will grow up to know you intimately for himself. Please help Barry and me to love him and prepare him to stand on his own with you." The next moments of silence felt holy, as if all I could do was rest in the presence of the Lord.

We look for spiritual moments in places where we think they should occur, as we gather to worship or as we kneel in prayer, but sometimes we are gifted—when it seems as if the Lord graciously allows his glory to visit our kitchen. Let us savor those moments when no one else can see us and nothing intrudes into our vision but Christ alone. Savor the moment and rest in him.

> *So I say to you, as the psalmist said to me today:*
> *Glorify the LORD with me; let us exalt his name together.*
>
> *Amen.*

AN UNUTTERABLE BEATITUDE

*Come, let us bow down in worship, let us kneel before
the LORD our Maker.*

PSALM 95:6

*B*arry faxed me a devotional thought from his desk calendar
today. It comes from the writings of A. W. Tozer:

> When the Holy Spirit is permitted to exercise his full
> sway in a redeemed heart there will likely be voluble praise
> first; then, when the crescendo rises beyond the ability of
> studied speech to express, comes song. When song breaks
> down under the weight of glory, then comes silence where
> the soul, held in deep fascination, feels itself blessed by an
> unutterable beatitude.

I was introduced to the writings of A. W. Tozer by my for-
mer boss at British Youth for Christ, Clive Calver—a committed Tozerite. We traveled all over the United Kingdom giving
church and citywide presentations on the power of prayer and
the impact of worship on the life of a city. I was a worship leader
and Clive would speak. We saw God move in some remarkable
ways, as ordinary men and women forgot about their lives and
worries for a while, caught up in waves of praise to the Lord. For
me the most memorable nights were when a silence would fall
on the worshipers. It was as if we could not move or say a word,
because we were on holy ground.

It's not very difficult to lead rousing worship; people love to
sing at the top of their lungs, particularly when there is a great
crowd and all are committed to the same purpose. But silence

before God is something else. It is as if you enter another room where words would be out of place and redundant.

I wonder if sometimes we gather for worship but leave too soon. We are encouraged by the volume of praise; it lifts our spirits, allowing us to lay aside our burdens for a while. But if we would wait, there is more. It is God's response to the worship of his children. An "unutterable beatitude" or blessing.

I watched one year as The Academy of Motion Pictures gave a special award to a veteran actor. Before he was invited to take the stage, we were treated to a brief overview of his prestigious career. Many of his industry colleagues praised his work. As he walked onto the stage the applause was deafening; he stood for a few moments enjoying the support of his community. Eventually the clapping subsided, but before he was able to make his speech the music played him off. *Sorry, time's up.* It was clear that he wanted to respond but the evening had moved on.

I think sometimes we do the same in our worship. We love to tell God how much we adore him, how he has changed our lives. We revel in the tidal waves of song, but then "time's up" and we move on. If we would just wait on God, let the silence fall, we could be gifted with the response of a loving Father to his children. In that holy moment we could receive a beatitude, a blessing that no human words could begin to frame.

> *A rising cloud of song, of music,*
> *soars above the crowd,*
> *lifted by the hearts and souls of those who gather now.*
> *But just beyond the doors of singing*
> *waiting for us all,*
> *the Father's hands upon our heads would fall.*
>
> *Amen.*

PART ELEVEN

JOY

The place God calls you to is the place where your deep gladness and the world's deep hunger meet.

FREDERICK BUECHNER,
WISHFUL THINKING

*H*e lived a small mean life. Those who knew sensed that with every deal he made he lost a piece of his soul, his humanity. He worked for the government and rationalized that everything he did was legal, but even he was not fooled by his defensive rhetoric.

He always took more than he should. He never looked you in the eye. All business deals were completed quickly, with no socializing. He knew that people talked about him. He saw them cross the street to avoid him, and for companionship he held his wallet a little closer.

He was on his way to collect a debt from an old woman— and eager to get it over with—when he saw a crowd of people gathered in the street. He tried to see what was happening, but the crowd was too big and he couldn't get a good view. He tried to push his way in, but no one would move for him. He took a few steps back and looked at the scene. To the left he saw a large tree that branched out over the center of the crowd. *Hmmm.* Tying his money belt a little tighter he began to climb.

He could hear a stranger's voice speaking to the assembled audience. Finally he cleared the top of the crowd and looked down at the speaker. His voice was strong and hypnotic. *What's he saying?* Suddenly the stranger stopped talking and looked up at him. He froze, having no desire to draw attention to himself while up a tree. The man began to speak: "Zacchaeus, come down immediately. I must stay at your house today."

The crowd began to mutter. "Doesn't Jesus know who this is?"

Zacchaeus climbed down the tree and waited, as the man who had called his name emerged from the crowd and walked with him to Zacchaeus's house.

Years later Zacchaeus still loved to tell the story to his friends, now numerous. His eyes always filled with tears as he remembered the day he moved from death to life. For the first time he felt loved, really loved.

What others remembered was what happened in the days following Jesus' house call. This man, whose greed and lust for power had kept him isolated from his community for years, suddenly changed.

People liked to tell their own stories. "He cheated me out of four pieces of silver and he came to see me the next day and gave me sixteen."

"Well, he didn't owe me anything, and yet he gave me enough to feed my family for a whole month. There is no one like Zacchaeus!"

I love this story. I love Christ's ability to see beyond our hard exteriors to the lonely souls inside and to call us by name. Salvation had come to Zacchaeus's home, and it showed in all sorts of ways. He didn't hug his new life to himself, accept that the past is the past, and move on; he wanted to make right the wrong he had done. But he went beyond that. He not only gave back generously to those he had cheated, but he also gave half of his considerable fortune to the poor. The joy of his new life met the poverty outside his door and did something about it. That is a true sign of a heart that is filled with gratitude to Christ: We become like him. We become gift givers. Salvation and a renewed soul are not gifts to be hugged to ourselves like universal secrets; they are to water our souls so that the whole world gets wet.

PURE JOY

Though you have not seen him, you love him; and
even though you do not see him now, you believe in him
and are filled with an inexpressible and glorious joy.

1 PETER 1:8

*T*his morning I had a long list of things to do. The house needed cleaning and our refrigerator was almost empty. I felt weighed down. I had been awake since four o'clock, wondering how we would take care of several things, turning them over and over in my mind and finding no immediate solution.

It used to be that when I felt that kind of anxiety grip my stomach, I would throw myself into everything, trying to make all the pieces fit. By the time my husband would come home from work, I would be as crazy as a starved pit bull.

Not anymore. Now I run away. "Okay, Bentley, we're out of here."

I pick up my golden retriever's leash and head for the car. His tail wags with wild abandon. I open the passenger door for him, and he jumps in. He takes his usual place sitting upright with his nose against the side window. As we get closer to the beach, I roll down his window so he can enjoy the fresh sea air and say hi to every passerby.

This being a weekday, I am able to find a parking spot close to the ocean. I take a deep breath of the salty air, cool for California. I stop to pick up a cup of coffee and fill B's bowl with water and then we head for the boardwalk. The surf is high and two young men in wet suits ride the waves with the passion of rodeo cowboys. I can see the outline of the island of Catalina like a cutout from a magazine pasted to the sky. An old man stops to talk to us: "Fine-looking dog you have!"

"Thanks," I reply. "His name is Bentley."

"Well, hi there, Wesley," he says.

Bentley licks his hand, prepared to let the name thing go.

"Used to have one of these myself," the man continues. "You get a lot of love from a dog. I had a cat first, but she was very stuck on herself."

I smile in agreement, thinking of my cat Abigail, who is indeed very stuck on herself.

"Saw a poster one day," he continues. "Picture of a big ol' ginger cat saying, 'If you want a friend, buddy, buy a dog.' So I did!" He walks away, laughing at his own joke. I wrap him in a prayer as I watch him shuffle down the boardwalk.

A toddler points to Bentley, and his mother brings him over to pat the dog's head. I hold B's collar. He is still a puppy, but at sixty-two pounds his enthusiasm could bowl a boy over. "What a beautiful little boy," I say to the woman.

"Thank you. We think so, too," she says with a warm smile. "We almost lost him when he was born. He is our little miracle." The little miracle sees a bird on the sand and is off for his next adventure.

I watch two children build a castle and think back to my childhood in Scotland. My brother, Stephen, and I used to build formidable forts and castles with intricate turrets and moats. I would decorate the walls with seashells, but of course our work of art was always gone the next morning. I would cry out in disappointment, seeing the little pile of shells alone on the sand. And then we would start all over again.

As I said, this morning I was running away. When life seems overwhelming, I've learned to take myself out of the situation, go to the ocean, and let God touch me. I don't take my list and pray over every item; I let God find me through old men and children and a waggy-tailed dog.

When I sit in despair at home, all I can see is myself and all the things that I need to do. When I weave myself into the tapestry of my town, I feel my selfish focus drift away. Sitting on the boardwalk, I think about the old man and wonder if he is alone. I make a mental note to look for him next time I am here. I think about that precious child gifted back to heartsick parents and pray that he will find his home in Christ at an early age. I consider the bird that evaded his sticky little hands; God knows its flight. I feel the companionship of Jesus. It's as if we are both smiling at the wonder and beauty of his work. I take a deep breath of the salty air. I know that my list still exists, but sitting here side by side with the Lord, I remember more important things. I remember his love, his grace, his timing.

Down on the sand the little boy runs to catch another bird and falls flat on his face. He is laughing, his mother is laughing, the bird is laughing, and so are my soul companion and I. I take another breath of the ocean spray. Joy is a gift.

In moments like these, as I watch the parade of life before my eyes, the emotion that sweeps over me goes far beyond happiness. It is pure joy.

When you welcome God's companionship in the darkest hours of your life, when you keep on walking by faith on the darker parts of the path, you are gifted with moments of wonderful elation—as if you are joining with heaven in a celebration that is a tiny shadow of what it will be like when we get home. The closer we push into the heart of God, the more we are swept away by the joy that is his breath and life and gift to us all.

Singing through the roaring ocean,
dancing on the crested waves,
all creation joins in telling
heaven's never-ending grace.
Sunshine spills across the water.
Seagulls rise on summer air.
Lord of Glory,
this your story
told to all who gather here.

A Grateful Heart

And he directed the people to sit down on the grass.
Taking the five loaves and the two fish and looking up to
heaven, he gave thanks and broke the loaves. Then he gave
them to the disciples, and the disciples gave them to the
people.

MATTHEW 14:19

*W*hat a day!" said Peter.

"I can't believe how long this crowd has stayed," Andrew added.

"They need to go home now. They're hungry, and I don't know about you, Andrew, but I am starving, and I've had enough of a crowd for one day. I'm going to tell Jesus to send them home."

Peter made his way through the vast crowd. Babies were crying. Children were chasing each other, jumping over unsuspecting adults. A few people had decided to take a nap on the hillside.

"Master, the people are hungry," Peter began. "I think you need to send them home now. I've had a look at their faces; they're exhausted. They need to eat."

"Then feed them, Peter," Jesus said. "Don't send them away."

Peter felt that old exasperation rise to the surface. This was such an impractical suggestion.

"We have five small loaves and two fish. Little fish," he said. "All we have is a boy's lunch, and you want us to feed this crowd?"

"Bring the food to me," Jesus answered.

Peter went back to where Andrew and the others were standing. "Is he going to send them away?" Andrew asked.

"No, he's not," Peter replied. "He wants us to feed them with a packed lunch."

"What?" Thomas exclaimed. "That's ridiculous."

"Just take the bread and fish to him," John said.

They all made their way through the people until they stood at Jesus' side.

"Here it is," said Peter, holding up a small parcel.

Jesus looked at the men and then lifted the tiny offering to heaven and said, "Thank you."

That is so radical to me! Imagine yourself in this position. Thousands of people are hungry. They are looking to you to feed them, and all you have is a tuna sandwich. At best, I can see myself on my face before God, begging him to do something. Jesus doesn't do that. He doesn't ask God to do anything. He just says, "Thank you." To me that says that his complete and utter trust is in God. It would have made no difference if a fast-food restaurant had suddenly appeared on the hillside, Christ's trust was in God, not in what shape the miracle took.

How wonderful to live in and with such confident gratitude. Can you imagine what a relief it would be? I spend so much time worrying about how things are going to work out rather than just giving thanks.

Barry and I rent a home. Today we received a letter telling us that we have to vacate the house three weeks before the baby is due. I look again at the life of Christ and I lift my eyes to heaven and I say, "Thank you."

Maybe you have a need that seems overwhelming. Try trusting God for his provision. Try looking up and saying thank you.

Joyful, joyful we adore thee,
God of glory, Lord of love!
Hearts unfold like flowers before thee,
Praising thee, their sun above.
Melt the clouds of sin and sadness,
Drive the dark of doubt away.
Giver of immortal gladness,
Fill us with the light of day.

HENRY VAN DYKE

Thank you, Lord, that you know our needs even before we speak a word. Help us to look to you with a grateful heart.

Amen.

LETTING GO

Do not be anxious about anything, but in everything, by prayer and petition, with thanksgiving, present your requests to God. And the peace of God, which transcends all understanding, will guard your hearts and your minds in Christ Jesus.

PHILIPPIANS 4:6–7

*W*hat a promise! This is an all-inclusive verse. Do not worry about anything. Don't worry about the children or your car payment or your job or your health. Whatever is on your heart and mind, bring it to the Lord in prayer and in petition and do it with thanksgiving. Thanksgiving is such an important part of the process because it speaks to trust and confidence.

Imagine that my car was broken down by the side of the road and two cars pulled over to help. The first driver who offers to look at the engine says he has no experience with cars; he's quite unmechanical—makes doughnuts for a living—but he's willing to take a look. The second driver is a car mechanic. I would be grateful to the first driver for stopping, but I wouldn't have any confidence in his ability to fix the problem. I'd rather he go for coffee and doughnuts than look under the hood! With the second driver I wouldn't just be grateful that he stopped; I would also have confidence that he knew what he was doing and that the end result would be favorable.

When we take our prayer requests to God and then continue to worry, it is as if we are saying, "Thanks so much for stopping to listen to me, but I'm not sure you can help." In our souls we sense the dissonance in that line of thinking. We believe that God is able to do what he says he will do, why then is it so difficult to rest in this promise that Paul brings before the church in Philippi? *Don't be anxious about anything.*

I think our need for control interferes with our trust in God. Joy and control do not make good roommates. I struggle with this daily. I've always found it hard to delegate. I figure if I do something myself then I know it will be done and done the way I think it should be. This spills over into my relationship with Christ. *Doing* makes me *feel* as if progress is being made—though that isn't necessarily so.

I face a number of situations that lack closure. I see clearly that I have two choices. I can bring these things to God and then spend the rest of the day trying to work out how I can "make things happen." Or I can bring my requests before God's throne of grace with a prayer of thanksgiving and confidence in him and wait on the Lord. The real difference is what happens in me after my initial prayer. If I make the first choice I continue to worry and fret over the outcome. If I take the second way, the way by which Paul exhorts us to live, I come to an awesome promise: "The peace of God, which transcends all understanding, will guard your hearts and your minds in Christ Jesus."

What a gift! The Word of God could not be clearer here. If we will relinquish control of our lives and place our trust in God with absolute confidence, then the peace of God, which is beyond human understanding, will cover us, protecting our hearts and minds. This is true joy. Joy that G. K. Chesterton called "the giant secret of the Christian."

Lord Jesus,
Today I choose to let go.
Today I choose to trust you.
Today I bring my life to you with thanksgiving,
my heart to you in prayer.
My questions I leave there.
Today I choose to let go.

Amen.

THE JOY OF COMFORT

Praise be to the God and Father of our Lord Jesus Christ, the Father of compassion and the God of all comfort, who comforts us in all our troubles, so that we can comfort those in any trouble with the comfort we ourselves have received from God.

2 CORINTHIANS 1:3–4

Second Corinthians 1:3–4 are two of my favorite verses of Scripture. They are a key piece in the jigsaw puzzle of our lives on this earth. Who among us can understand all the things that happen that cause us pain and grief? There are so many unanswered questions, so many pieces of the puzzle that we don't have. But what we do have is the privilege of sharing with others the fruit of our struggle. What God has given us we have the joy of sharing with each other.

I have just returned from a wonderful women's conference in Cocoa Beach, Florida. The weekend theme was "Out of the shadows, into the light." On Friday evening I spoke about my own life, my battle with clinical depression and what I have learned about its roots. I told them how God helped me deal with anger, shame, and fear, and about the joy that comes from living in the light, no longer trying to hide from God, ourselves, or each other. I could see recognition in the eyes of the women. We broke for coffee and sat around our tables and began to talk. I know only what happened at my table, but I'm sure the pattern was duplicated all across the room. One by one the women opened up to each other and talked about their lives, their struggles, questions, and fears. I sat and listened. Someone said, "I went through that and here's what God taught me." And another: "I know how painful that is; I would love to help you." Or, "Just hold on, it will get much easier."

God has been so faithful to me—not only restoring joy, but also bringing a new depth of joy that I had never before tasted. When you face your greatest fears and Christ meets you in the middle of that place and walks you through every step of the way, life is richer than anything *Money* magazine can dream up.

The added joy is in bringing hope and comfort to others. As the body of Christ, we don't exist for ourselves but for Christ and for one another, for a world that has lost all hope. When the Lord restores our souls, it's only natural that we turn to those around us who are broken and bleeding and put an arm around them and walk beside them. This is what I saw in those women. They reached through the walls of their own lives and brought each other comfort and hope. Many painful but healing tears were shed that weekend.

Joy is not an escape from pain; it is a recognition in the midst of it that we have a God of all comfort who never leaves us nor forsakes us. True joy has little to do with self and all to do with the goodness and mercy of God. And the stories we have to tell along the way are like diamonds shining a path through the night.

Comfort, comfort my people, says your God. Speak tenderly to Jerusalem, and proclaim to her that her hard service has been completed, that her sin has been paid for, that she has received from the LORD's hand double for all her sins. A voice of one calling: "In the desert prepare the way for the LORD; make straight in the wilderness a highway for our God. Every valley shall be raised up, every mountain and hill made low; the rough ground shall become level, the rugged places a plain. And the glory of the LORD will be revealed, and all mankind together will see it. For the mouth of the LORD has spoken."

ISAIAH 40:1–5

JOY TO THE WORLD

Suddenly a great company of the heavenly host appeared with the angel, praising God and saying, "Glory to God in the highest, and on earth peace to men on whom his favor rests."

LUKE 2:13

*I*t's cold tonight," Samuel said.

"But look how clear the stars are," his friend John pointed out. "It's as if you could reach up and touch them."

Samuel threw some more wood on the fire and got up to stretch his old legs. The sheep were grazing in the moonlight. It was a quiet night.

"I'm hungry," John said. "Do we have anything else to eat?"

"Here, catch!" Simon had been going through their provisions with the same thought in mind and he threw John a loaf of bread.

"It's nice to be up here away from all the noise of the town tonight," Samuel said. "I've never seen Bethlehem so busy. I can't stand all that pushing and shoving!"

John laughed. "It's *people* you can't stand. If they don't have four legs and a wooly coat, you've got no time for them!"

Samuel grunted something about "no respect" and wandered over to the side of the hill. It was quiet, so quiet, almost unnaturally so.

"What's up, old man?" Simon asked.

"I don't know," he replied. "It's too quiet tonight."

All three men stood still for a moment and listened. There was a hush over the hillside like the silence that falls just before someone begins to tell a story.

Suddenly into the stillness burst the brightest light that Samuel had ever seen in his seventy-four years on the hills. "What is it?" cried John.

No one replied, as terror had robbed them of the power of speech. Then an angel appeared before them. And a voice, a voice such as they had never heard before, pierced the night. "Do not be afraid. I bring you good news of great joy that will be for all the people. Today in the town of David a Savior has been born to you; he is Christ the Lord. This will be a sign to you: You will find a baby wrapped in cloths and lying in a manger" (Luke 2:10–12).

Before they could even begin to take in the message of this glorious figure, he was surrounded by others like him and they were all singing. Joy! Joy! Joy! The song shook the hillside. The shepherds were on their knees by now, terror-struck, awestruck. They knew that this was a moment like none other in history, and they were there. They were there!

That declaration of joy to the world changed everything for you and me—forever. Up until that moment men and women struggled on, the best they could, to live a holy life in an unholy world. But it was never enough. Then, into this cold faithless world, God sent his Son, a Savior.

To this day we rejoice over many things, but none like this. Into the world of Samuel's old bones and John's rumbling stomach came hope for us all. Christ is born! Peace has come! Joy to the world!

Joy to the world, the Lord is come!
Let earth receive her King;
Let every heart prepare him room,
And heaven and nature sing.

ISAAC WATTS

PART TWELVE

PILGRIMS

Stand at the crossroads and look; ask for the ancient paths, ask where the good way is, and walk in it, and you will find rest for your souls.

JEREMIAH 6:16

A message I heard on a daily radio broadcast called "Come Up Higher" has had a deep impact on me. The question was asked: "Are we tourists or pilgrims on this earth?"

Think about it. The obvious and correct answer is that, as Christians, we are pilgrims. But if we examine the profile of both types of travelers, I wonder which our lives would actually line up with. My dictionary defines a *pilgrim* as "one who embarks on a quest for something conceived of as sacred." Under *tourist* it says, "One who travels for pleasure."

Pilgrims are on a mission; they are going somewhere, no matter what the cost. This journey is their destiny in life, their reason for being. Their energy and attention is focused on the truth that they are going somewhere, not anywhere, but somewhere in particular.

Tourists, on the other hand, have the luxury of choice. If they had planned to go one way and the weather turns bad or the currency rate changes, they can change their minds and go somewhere else, somewhere more pleasing to themselves or their circumstances. Much of their time is taken up seeing the sights, being in all of the right places at the right time. It is a self-driven endeavor.

It is so easy today to live as spiritual tourists, reading the right books, going to the right conferences. We can choose to live with great conviction—until the weather changes and it doesn't feel as good anymore. So then we cancel part of our trip and rest awhile. If we view ourselves as tourists, we will become discouraged when things don't go the way we had hoped, when the scenery is not as spectacular as the brochure promised. A tourist venture is largely a selfish thing, to make us happy.

A pilgrim does not have that luxury. We do not have that luxury. As pilgrims our expectations are different. We are going somewhere because we have been called there and no other place will do. We don't expect it always to be safe or comfortable, but it is not about us or what makes us happy. A tourist has a fistful of postcards and Kodak moments, but a pilgrim has a heart full of faith and love and commitment to a higher calling.

> *O God, our help in ages past,*
> *Our hope for years to come,*
> *Be thou our guide while life shall last,*
> *And our eternal home.*
>   ISAAC WATTS

CHRISTIAN

*I have fought the good fight, I have finished the race,
I have kept the faith.*

2 TIMOTHY 4:7

$\mathcal{W}$e picked a table by the window in our favorite coffee-and-book store and settled in to do some serious work. Barry had three what-to-name-the-baby books and I had two.

"What do you think of the name Elliot?" I asked.

"No, I don't think so," he replied. "What about Taylor?"

"Taylor Pfaehler, are you kidding?" We both laughed and went back to our respective books.

"What are some good Scottish names?" Barry asked.

"Well, there's Ian, but we can't name him after my brother-in-law. There's Rory or Colin or Stewart or Fergus or Ewan."

"Okay, back to the books," he said.

Two mugs of coffee, two Cokes, and one bowl of potato-and-leek soup later, we had our son's name. We both knew that it was absolutely the right name for our little boy: Christian. John Bunyan's pilgrim.

"Let's buy him the book," I said. "I want him to know the story for himself."

We paid for our drinks and wandered over to children's books. "It'll be in the classics section—if they have a children's edition," I said. "Yes, here it is!" Later that evening we sat and read some of the story together. "This is great, Barry. It's beautifully illustrated and simplified, and we'll be able to read it to him when he is a little boy."

The next day, when Barry was at work, I took outside the abridged version of John Bunyan's *Pilgrim's Progress* and I read that familiar, wonderful story. I wrote these words inside the front cover:

> This is for you, little lamb. Your father and I want you to know that life is a journey home. There will be good things and bad things happen to you but if you will learn at an early age to put your trust in Christ and keep on walking, you will live up to your name. You don't belong to your dad and me, but we will be your companions on the road every step of the way. I don't know whom you will look like or what you will do with your life, but if you are able to say that you have run the race and kept the faith, then your life will have been well lived. We love you, Christian Walsh Pfaehler.

Set your inner compass on the road that leads you home,
over rocks that bruise and tear
through the night when no one's there.
Live your life a constant prayer,
Christian, walk on home.

FOOTPRINTS IN THE SAND

In the desert . . . you saw how the LORD your God carried you, as a father carries his son, all the way you went until you reached this place.

DEUTERONOMY 1:31

*W*hen I was visiting a dear friend, she asked me to read a card she'd received from her son. He had gone through a difficult time and had sent this card to let his parents know that he was fine, that his trust was still in the Lord. The message included the "Footprints" poem. I'd read it before but now was reminded again of the tender compassion of God toward a weary pilgrim.

The traveler in the poem has just walked through a difficult patch. He turns around and is confused and hurt to see only one set of footprints in the sand. Hadn't Christ promised to walk beside him all the way? The Lord replies, explaining that the one set of prints is Jesus'—he had been carrying the traveler like a child.

For years this poem was printed as being by "Anonymous." But there's a real author behind the lines, and the poem providentially "came back" to encourage her family at a time of real crisis. Margaret Fishback Powers wrote "Footprints" as a young woman afraid of what troubles might lie ahead. She lost track of the poem and didn't hear those words again for twenty years. Then they came to her just when she needed them. After a serious accident, her daughter lay in a Canadian hospital fighting for her very survival. Seeing his daughter's injuries, Margaret's husband suffered a heart attack and was admitted to the same hospital. A nurse read him a poem, saying, "I don't know who wrote this, but I hope it will encourage you not to give up hope." He listened to those words of promise wash over him and said, "My wife wrote that poem twenty years ago."

"Footprints" is not just a beautiful poem written by a young woman comforted in her walk with God. The poem captures the heart of God toward us: "You saw how the LORD your God carried you, as a father carries his son, all the way you went until you reached this place."

God understands that we are not strong all the time. Sometimes all we can do is rest in his arms as he takes us the next few miles. Things happen to us that break our hearts; our legs may buckle under us. But we are not left lying by the side of the road like a failed runner counted out of the race. When our trust is in Christ and our hearts are committed to our journey home, the One who walks beside us bends and gently picks us up and carries us for a while.

Lord,
Thank you that when I am weak you carry me.
Thank you that when I am sad you comfort me.
Thank you that when I am lost you shelter me.
Thank you that in all of this, you love me.

Amen.

THE HEART OF A PILGRIM

I tell you, my friends, do not be afraid of those who kill the body and after that can do no more.

LUKE 12:4

*H*ello, stranger!" I said. "I haven't talked to you in a while." I was pleasantly surprised when I picked up the phone and heard the voice of my friend Cher Nelson.

"I've just returned from China," she said.

"Oh! How was your trip?" I asked.

"Absolutely amazing!" she replied. "I have never encountered Christians like the Chinese believers."

"Tell me about them," I said.

"It's their utter devotion to Christ that stays with me," she began. "They told us not to bother praying for a change in government. They belong to another kingdom. One of the pastors asked us not to pray for things to get easier for them, because it would be more difficult to be faithful without persecution."

"How do they handle being persecuted for their faith?" I asked.

"They accept suffering as part of the Christian life," she said. "They say the Bible teaches that we will be persecuted if we follow Christ—so they just accept it. They ask for prayer—that they will be faithful in their suffering."

"Can you describe some of the 'pictures' you have brought back with you?" I asked.

"I can still see smashed hands and broken arms that have healed badly, some of the Christians having been beaten and tortured. But they pay no attention to these things," she answered.

"All they care about is that by God's grace they will be faithful. I noticed that they wanted to *hear* us pray. And they don't care what denomination you are from; they just want to know if you love Jesus."

Long after we said good-bye I continued to think about what Cher said. I can't imagine what it is like to be continuously persecuted for your faith in Christ. And then to think that their number-one prayer request is that they will be faithful. If I were in a situation like that, I think my daily prayer would be that the suffering would stop.

These our brothers and sisters in Christ have pilgrim hearts. They have no fear of what man can do to their bodies; their only fear is of the Lord. Would that God would give each and every one of us the heart of a pilgrim.

Give me the heart of a pilgrim,
steadfast and loyal and true.
Help me to fly like an arrow
focused on no one but you.
Lord, may my fear be of you alone and my life reflect your
love.

Amen.

NEVER TOO LATE

Rejoice in the Lord always. I will say it again: Rejoice!

PHILIPPIANS 4:4

I smiled when I read the poster in the window of the mall beauty salon: "It's never too late to be what you might have been." It was surrounded by pictures of the latest hairstyles and colors. I guess that was supposed to be the message: It's never too late to be a blond if that's what you know you are deep inside! The quote was attributed to George Eliot, author of the classic *Silas Marner*. I'm not sure that's how Eliot intended the quote to be used, but I think it's a wonderful statement and a spiritual truth. In God it's never too late to be what you might have been. So many people walk through life with regret. That seems such a wasted, draining emotion to me. We are not powerless in our lives to make change, to start over again, to learn to do better next time.

I recently read a wonderful poem by Hugh Prather, from his book *Notes to Myself,* that captured this thought so beautifully:

> *If I had only forgotten future greatness*
> *and looked at the green things and the buildings*
> *and reached out to those around me*
> *and smelled the air*
> *and ignored the forms and the self-styled obligations*
> *and heard the rain on the roof*
> *and put my arms around my wife*
> *and it's not too late.*

There is so much in life that is wonderful, and it's not too late to grab hold of it. It's not too late to be kind, it's not too late to be loving, it's not too late to tell the truth, to be honest. It's not too late to walk by the ocean, it's not too late to pray, it's not too late to tell your children that you love them, it's not too late to tell the Lord that you love him.

It's not too late to be what you might have been.
I saw myself a prisoner to all the things I've been.
I saw the play repeat itself reliving every scene.
But then I heard a voice that said step out and choose again,
step out and live, step out and love,
be what you might have been.

Thank you, Lord,
Amen.

COME HOME

What good is it for a man to gain the whole world,
and yet lose or forfeit his very self?

LUKE 9:25

*O*ne of my most treasured books is *Beside the Bony Brier Bush* by Ian Maclaren. I have an old copy first owned by a George Seull in 1898 and gifted to me by Ruth Graham. I love the stories told in true Scottish brogue—seven stories, all with a message of deep spiritual truth. As Ian walks the reader through the highlands, I can see the heather and the bright yellow gorse bushes and the fields of bluebells waving in the wind. But the story that I go back to over and over again is about Lachlan Campbell and his daughter Flora.

Lachlan was a hard man, a devout believer who held the scales of justice tightly with little mercy or grace. One evening he brought a case of discipline before the church board. A young girl, he explained, had left home for the evils of London; she wasn't expected to be seen again. He came with a recommendation: that her name—the name of his own daughter, Flora—be struck off the church roll. The men in the fellowship were heartbroken for Lachlan. But they refused his recommendation; they would not take Flora's name off the role, saying, "In the Lord there is mercy and with him is plenteous redemption."

Lachlan stood before them in silence, and the minister took the broken man to his house. He sat Lachlan by the fire and like a father asked him to explain what had happened. Lachlan pulled out a letter from Flora in which she poured out her heart, asking her father to forgive her for running away—but she could no longer live by his strict standards. "Perhaps," she said, "if my mother had lived she would have understood me. My greatest regret, Father, is that I will never see you again in this world or the next."

"That's not the letter of a bad girl," said the minister kindly. "Just a sad one."

Lachlan got up to leave. "You won't take her name off the church role, but I've taken her name out of the family Bible."

For some time his neighbors in Drumtochty watched lonely, solitary Lachlan come and go until one woman could hold herself back no longer. Marget knocked on his door and told Lachlan that she had come in the name of the Lord to tell him that the family shame was his and not his daughter's. "Where would we be," she said, "if God had turned his back on us as you have on your own daughter?"

With those words God pierced this proud man's heart. Marget sat down with him and wrote to Flora, telling her to come home; her father was waiting for her with arms open wide. Every night as Lachlan went to bed he left a light burning in the window—in case it was the night that Flora came home.

And one night she did. It was dark as she made her way toward her father's house. She was so afraid. She knew her father and his iron principles well. Finally through the woods she saw the cottage; it was ablaze with light, and she understood. Running to the door, she was too overwhelmed to knock or speak, but her father knew she had come, because the dogs, who had never forgotten her or written her off, barked for joy. Lachlan opened the door. Though he had never kissed his daughter in all her twenty years, he gathered her in his arms and kissed her. That night they opened the family Bible together and wrote,

Flora Campbell, missed April 1873
Found September 1873.
"Her father fell on her neck and kissed her."

Perhaps as you read these words you see yourself in Flora. In leaving her father's home for the big city, she was turning away also from his faith. I talk to many people who have lost the way home. Perhaps raised by strict, unbending parents, they throw their own faith away as they reject a standard that they feel is crushing them. My question is always the same: "Did you find what you were looking for?"

Perhaps you see yourself in Lachlan Campbell. Refusing to bend or compromise, you have written someone off. You have said, "I have no daughter. I have no son." Where would we be if God had done that to us?

As I close this book I present challenges to any would-be pilgrim or weary pilgrim: If you have lost your way and you have lost hope, come home. The Father is waiting for you. It doesn't matter where you have been. All that matters is where you are going. And for those who have hardened hearts against someone, those who march on toward heaven without ever looking back, I hold up the picture of a father standing at the window, never letting the light go out. I challenge you to reach out and to wait and pray and love—for today could be the day a child returns home.

Thank you, Lord, that you have never given up on me.
I set my feet and my heart toward home.

Amen.

If you are interested in having Sheila Walsh speak at your church, conference, or special event, please contact her office at:

P.O. Box 150783
Nashville, TN 37215
(615) 463-2626